Your Path To Unshakeable Happiness

Practical Modern Day Buddhism

2nd Edition

Margaret Blaine

A & M Publishing
Eugene, Oregon
www.margaretblaine.com

Cover and Book Design
by
Arden W. Munkres

ISBN-13: 978-1477651148

"Our lives are infinitely precious. Not to attain a state of absolute happiness in this lifetime is a great loss. Our Buddhist practice exists so we can attain indestructible happiness."
Daisaku Ikeda

Faith Into Action, p. 37

Acknowledgements

It takes a community to bring a book to fruition and I want to express my appreciation to all the people who helped me with this one.

My deepest gratitude goes to my mentor and teacher Daisaku Ikeda, who taught me the heart of Buddhism through his example. Also to the wonderful SGI members who have nurtured and befriended me from day one.

Particular thanks to Linda Clare, my writing teacher, who has been so patient and encouraging. She has taught me in classes, listened to this book for five years in her critique group, and was my first editor.

My heartfelt thanks to my critique group. They made sure I wrote a book they could understand, as they are unfamiliar with Buddhism. They were rigorous in this endeavor and the book is much better for it.

My special appreciation to my husband, Arden Munkres, a graphic designer, who designed the cover, then formatted and edited the book. Over the years he has supported my creative process. I couldn't have written this book without him.

My thanks to Greg Martin, a leader in the SGI, who read the book, made sure I was correct in my presentation of Buddhist principles, and wished me well.

My gratitude to my sister Skye and my brother-in-law Boudewijn and Heather McBride who spent many hours editing this book.

Table of Contents

1: The Purpose of Buddhist Practice............ **Page 1**
To the Reader 5
Establishing Unshakeable Happiness–
Enlightenment

2: The Buddha Nature 9
To the Reader 13
Discovering Your Buddha Nature

3: Oneness of Self and Environment................... 15
To the Reader 19
You Are One With Your Environment

4: The Ten Worlds: the Lower Six....................... 23
To the Reader 27
Identifying Internal States

5: Adverse Circumstances Lead to Growth 29
To the Reader 37
Using Obstacles to Grow

6: Relative Versus Unshakeable Happiness 39
To the Reader 43
Growing Happiness From the Inside Out

7: Introduction to Buddhist Practice................... 45
To the Reader 55
Setting Goals

8: Change Brings Resistance 59
To the Reader 65
Using the Chant to Overcome Resistance

9: Poison Into Medicine 67
To the Reader 73
Turning Around Adverse Circumstances

10: The Start of the Experiment 77
To the Reader 83
Chanting at Home

11: The Ten Worlds: The Four Higher Worlds ... 87
To the Reader 95
Using the Chant to Change Your Life Condition

12: Obstacles Are Steps on the Path 99
To the Reader 107
Chanting to Overcome Obstacles

13: Changing Karma 111
To the Reader 115
Changing Circumstances From the Inside Out

14: Steps to Happiness 119
To the Reader 127
Becoming Happy Might Require Change

15: Tap Into Your Buddha Nature 129
To the Reader: 135
Practicing for Self and for Others

16: Why Does This Keep Happening, Anyway? 137
To the Reader 149
Understanding The Simultaneity of Cause and
Effect

17: Twists and Turns: Never Give Up 153
To the Reader 165
Chanting for as Long as It Takes

18: Benefits and Self Knowledge 169
To the Reader 173
Realizing Earthly Desires Can Lead to an
Awakening

19: The Ninety-day Experiment Continues....... 177
To the Reader 183
Handling Doubts

20: A Crisis and Growth.................................. 187
To the Reader 195
Chanting to Change Your Karma

21: Lessons, Lessons, Lessons 197
To the Reader 201
Tumbling the Taro

22: Chanting Leads to Action.............................. 205
To the Reader 211
Learning About Human Revolution

23: Who Said It Would Be Easy? 215
To the Reader 221
Modifying Your Behavior

24: Fundamental Darkness.................................. 225
To the Reader 229
Discovering That Life Is a Mirror

25: See the Truth of the Matter 233
To the Reader 239
Using the Strategy of the Lotus Sutra

26: Steps of Human Revolution........................... 243
To the Reader 249
Taking Your Life Into Your Hands

27: A Crucial Moment... 251
To the Reader 259
Chanting in a Crucial Moment

28: Make a Determination to Win....................... 263
To the Reader 269
Handling a Difficult Person

viii

29: You Are a Buddha, Not a Beggar.................. 273
To the Reader 277
Understanding Cause and Effect

30: A Big Leap Takes Courage 287
To the Reader 285
Hope Versus Determination

31 One Step At a time... 287
To the Reader 291
Standing Strong Against the Eight Winds

32: Chant and Never Be Deadlocked.................. 293
To the Reader 299
Faith Equals Daily Life

33: Who Would Have Believed It!........................ 303
To the Reader 307
Receiving The Gohonzon

34: An Aftermath and a Beginning 309
To the Reader 313
Summarizing the Main Points

Bibliography 317

How to find Us.. 319

Introduction

Are you facing a crossroads and searching for a path to your new life? Maybe you're trying to find a way to make your life sing, or you're just a curious person who likes to try new things.

Whatever your motivation, this book is dedicated to guiding you through the process of constructing a life full of satisfaction and joy. You'll learn how to overcome life's hardships and build a core of unshakeable happiness through a Buddhist chanting practice.

You will be introduced to the story of Nancy and Doug. They're obliged to engage with real world issues as we all must. You'll acquaint yourself with the steps to building a happy life, as Nancy and Doug learn to chant from practitioners. You will also see how the practice works as they grapple with their problems and begin to turn their lives in the direction of happiness.

This book will show you how to start the chanting practice yourself by trying the ninety-day experiment shown in the *To The Reader* sections at the end of each chapter.

You will discover that Nichiren Buddhism is a practical way of life, not a traditional religion. It is a hands-on path to taking charge of your life and is a prove-it-to-yourself practice. You prove it by seeing whether you get results.

How do I know you can find unshakeable happiness? Because I've not only used the practice myself, but have been in contact with and heard the experiences of hundreds of people who have also used it to live progressive, satisfying lives.

You don't have to believe anything when you begin. Just be willing to try something new and stick with it for ninety days. Don't hesitate if you have doubts. Doubts are normal at this stage.

Do enjoy the adventure. I say adventure because when you start to chant you will be surprised and fascinated by what happens in your life. So, let's begin.

The Purpose of Buddhist Practice

On a winter evening in Eugene, Oregon, at least fifty people attended an introductory Buddhist meeting at the Soka Gakkai International (SGI) community center. Nancy Robertson waited to speak. She was due to give an experience to the group, describing what had happened in her life as the result of Buddhist practice, as she had been chanting for twenty years. Changes had taken place during those years, which had transformed every aspect of her life.

The emcee introduced her and Nancy rose to her feet. She was a slender, forty-year-old woman, with naturally curly brown hair. Cut short, it showed off the graceful shape of her head. Her penetrating blue eyes were serene as she turned to the audience with confidence, back straight, her head held high.

"I've been asked to share with you what's happened in my life as a result of practicing Nichiren Daishonin's Buddhism." She paused and looked around the room. "To be honest with you, when I began, I didn't think I would ever be standing here to talk about my life." The audience rustled as people settled in to listen. She looked around, noting that there were probably fifteen newcomers in the crowd.

"When I was introduced to the practice, I had serious problems. I was living with my boyfriend and our life together wasn't going well. He was drinking too much and we had many fights, which were escalating over time. My life was not happy and I didn't know what to do to change it." She smiled at them, her gaze sweeping the audience.

"My sponsor, the person who introduced me, told me that this practice exists for my happiness as it does for yours as well. We should all be able to overcome the problems in our lives and create our lives as we want them."

Nichiren Daishonin, the founder of this branch of Buddhism, promised us that we can all lead victorious lives. In a letter to one of his followers, entitled *Reply to Kyo'o*, he said:

> *"This sutra, the Lotus Sutra, can fulfill their desires, as a clear cool pond can satisfy all those who are thirsty. They will enjoy peace and security in their present existence and good circumstances in future existences."*
>
> *Writings of Nichiren Daishonin,* p. 412

She paused. One younger woman, arms folded defensively across her chest, wore a prove-it-to-me look on her face. Nancy wondered who had brought her. She concluded it was probably the young man beside her, who kept glancing her way. Another older woman looked tired, yet her eyes had hope.

Nancy continued. "I didn't know what to believe. All I knew was something in my life had to change if I was ever going to become happy. Then my sponsor told me that I didn't have to believe anything, that each of us proves to him or her self whether this Buddhism works. I decided that since I didn't know what else to do, that I would try it, just to see if it worked. Like an experiment."

Nancy glanced at her best friend, Hanako, who stood in the back, smiling and nodding. "Not everyone will have the experience I did, but once I put my feet on this path I've stayed with it ever since. I can guarantee that if you decide to try it, after hearing my experience, your life will become an adventure."

She caught the frown of a man in the second row. Speaking directly to him, she said, "I imagine I can guess what you're thinking. You're wondering if this is all just wishful thinking."

Both he and the young woman actually nodded in agreement. The older woman looked more hopeful, not quite so defeated.

Sharing her message made Nancy feel energized. "I attended a meeting one night where the members described how happiness had come into their lives. Every person there had become happy, just as predicted. 'Happiness comes in like the tide,' they said. This was my experience too. At first they were somewhat happier. Then happiness would ebb, like the tide going out. When the next wave came in, happiness stayed longer and grew deeper. So it grew, widening and deepening until everyone stayed happy no matter what."

The young woman seemed to have settled down. Her arms, which had been folded across her chest, had relaxed into her lap.

Nancy held up a hand. "This didn't happen overnight. We had to learn to be consistent in doing the daily practice. We had to take action, face our fears and change our behavior. But *anyone* who is willing to do these things can change his or her life for the better, even those with the most difficult circumstances."

4

A hand went up in the back, a man about forty, Nancy guessed. "You're saying that it's possible to overcome difficult problems?" He sounded skeptical.

Nancy nodded. "That's exactly my experience. Remember, you don't have to believe me. I don't expect anyone to believe what I say at this point. I just hope that you will listen with an open mind."

"My story is also partly Doug's story. I'd like to introduce you to him since he is a large part of this time in my life." She motioned to Doug. He rose. Nancy noted his color was good and he appeared healthy. He looked a lot better than he had when they were together.

♦

As Doug walked across the front of the room to the mike he brushed back his bangs which tended to fall over his eyes. He looked across the audience and saw the weariness and skepticism on some of their faces.

"I want to welcome all of you tonight. During the period of time when Nancy and I were together, I was young and very skeptical of the practice, as some of you might be tonight. Sometimes people try the practice to prove that it won't work as I did." He paused smiling ruefully. "No one is asking you to believe anything. You will decide for yourself. This is enough from me for now. This is Nancy's experience." He walked back to his seat, handing Nancy the mike as he passed her.

♦

Nancy saw the beginning of some smiles in the audience. "I guess I was more hopeful than Doug and more willing to try something new." As she took a deep breath preparing to begin, she hoped her story would help others give the practice a try.

To the Reader

Establishing Unshakeable Happiness– Enlightenment

In the last chapter, we met Nancy after she'd been practicing Buddhism for twenty years. In the following chapters, we are going to go back twenty years in time and examine what Nancy's life was like when she began her practice.

Nancy's life is an amalgamation of the kinds of experiences gleaned from different practitioners. The purpose of this book is to show you how the practice can work in the life of one individual. All of us cope with problems in life and the issues you might be dealing with may not be the same as hers. That doesn't matter. These characters, Nancy and Doug, will show you how any problem can be overcome in your own life by using Nichiren Daishonin's chanting practice. You, too, can become happy.

There is no question that Nichiren Buddhism is a pathway to happiness. The lives of all those who practice experienced a turn-around. Initially, everyone struggled with problems, and then were able to turn those obstacles around and overcome them, finding success in life. This has happened with all different kinds of issues, including financial, health, and relationship difficulties.

So what does happiness mean anyway? Some people think happiness means never having problems. But, think about it. Is this truly realistic? Challenges come up over and over in life, as we all know. They're part of everyone's life.

Is happiness fulfilling every wish and desire? There's no question that getting what we want can provide short-term happiness, but inevitably, after time passes, we start looking for more. This kind of happiness is temporary and I think most of us want a happiness that is not going to disappear after a period of time.

To a Buddhist, happiness means to experience the profound joy that comes from never being defeated by problems in life. When you know you can overcome difficulties as they come up, something subtle and profound happens. A surety and confidence expands deep in your life, and you come to know that there is nothing to worry about.

In Buddhism, as taught by Nichiren Daishonin, practitioners use their life challenges as a catalyst to deepen and expand their inner lives, to manifest life's highest potentials such as wisdom, courage, vitality and compassion, and to live life with a deeper and stronger sense of hope, confidence and appreciation.

Ultimately, as you connect with and develop faith in that inner level of life, happiness expands and deepens in your life and comes to underlie any disruptions and upsets on the outer level of life.

Recently, a practitioner of four months shared her experience. When she encountered the practice she was struggling with severe financial problems. She took chanting on with determination and started to overcome the financial difficulties. Even though the problems still come up, she's happy for the first time in fifteen years.

After experiencing what has happened in their lives and in the lives of many, many others, practitioners want to introduce as many of you as possible to the practice, so you too may have the same experience of fulfillment in life and become absolutely happy.

You don't have to be nervous. Everyone is his own final judge as to whether this Buddhism is right for them. The hope is that after reading this book you will want to experiment with this "prove it to yourself" practice and see what happens in your life. Buddhism is always reasonable. It is not reasonable to expect someone to believe in something when they don't know if it will work in their life. So, let's begin and see what happens to Nancy.

2

The Buddha Nature

Twenty Years Earlier

The door to the Family Service agency restroom opened and a perky triangular face topped by a mop of short, tousled black hair peered in. "There you are! I've been looking for you."

Nancy looked up, knowing her face looked puffy and red. Although Lisa was her friend, she was also her co-worker. Nancy didn't like to be seen crying at work. "Hi Lisa," she said wearily. "Is Annette looking for me again?"

Lisa nodded. "Fraid so."

Nancy sighed. Annette was their supervisor at the agency where Nancy and Lisa handled the front office. Annette was very ambitious, micromanaging her workers to make herself look good to Sue, the head of the social work department. Over the year Nancy had worked there, she and Lisa had developed a friendship and looked out for one another.

Annette was beautiful. She had creamy skin and wore her smooth black hair pulled over her ears into a chignon. She always looked sleek, dressing in form fitting clothes. When Nancy'd first met her, she'd felt an intuitive shock. Annette was a shark! Then noting that she limped and needed a cane, Nancy had felt some sympathy, but she was always cautious around her boss.

Annette's piercing black eyes didn't miss much. She didn't like it when one of them took too much time out of the office outside their usual break time. Just last week Nancy had been called to Annette's office and given a reprimand.

Nancy blew her nose and wiped her eyes, trying to hide the fact she had been crying.

Lisa's smile turned to a frown. "What's the matter, honey?"

"It's nothing."

"Oh come on, Nancy. You've been crying."

Nancy had to talk to someone. Hiding what was going on at home certainly hadn't changed anything, and she knew she could trust Lisa to keep silence in the office. If you wanted your reputation shredded just let something out there. It would be all over the agency in twenty-four hours.

Nancy took a deep breath. "I had a big fight with Doug last night. I questioned some decision he made and he blew up and now he won't talk to me. And, that's not all. We used to drink wine on the weekends but now he's drinking too much bourbon in the evenings, and he changes when he drinks. He loses his temper and gets really impatient. I'm almost afraid of him." Tears flowed again.

"Oh honey." Lisa put her arm around Nancy. "You were so happy when you moved in with him."

"I know I was!" The words poured out in a rush. "We had so much fun together. We laughed a lot. We loved hiking in the mountains, and biking along the river.

We'd take walks at Fifth Street Market looking in shop windows, just talking. He took me out to dinner. The drinking wasn't a problem then." She looked at Lisa for understanding and received a reassuring smile.

"He understood me in a way my family never did. And Lisa, he was sweet. I'm so confused. I miss the Doug I moved in with. I want him back." Nancy put her face in her hands and sobbed. Lisa held her and murmured soothing words.

After a few minutes, Lisa stepped back and handed Nancy a washcloth. "You need to get some cold water on your face before we go back to the front office." Nancy nodded through her tears. She couldn't stay away any longer. She couldn't afford to lose this job.

Then Lisa paused and gave Nancy a speculative look. "Before we go back, I've got something to tell you. I decided to share this with you this because you've been so unhappy at work." Uncharacteristically, she hesitated.

Nancy waited for her to continue. She glanced into the mirror. Her nose was pink and her face blotchy. I look awful, she thought. Nancy patted cold water on her face, waiting. When the silence continued, she turned to look at Lisa, and saw her take a deep breath.

"I've started going to a Buddhist center, founded by a man named Nichiren Daishonin. The people there do a chant and their lives seem to work better. I think mine is starting to change too, although I haven't been doing it for very long."

"You're saying that you chant and you think your life is working better?" Nancy looked at Lisa with surprise. That sounded kind of wacky. It wasn't like Lisa to be wacky. She'd always seemed to have her feet on the ground.

"Yes, that's exactly it," said Lisa. "Why don't you come with me to a meeting for new people and let the more experienced ones explain it?"

Nancy considered the offer. She was so tired all the time now and once she got home it would be hard to leave with Doug wanting her home all of the time during his time off. It would be too much hassle for something that didn't seem to make much sense.

"I'll pass," she said.

Lisa looked disappointed but seemed to accept her answer. "If you ever change your mind, just let me know," she said. Nancy nodded.

"Okay. I'm going back now. I'll try to distract Annette." Lisa opened the door and left.

While Nancy washed her face, she reflected on what she hadn't told Lisa. She hadn't mentioned Doug's possessiveness. It had gotten much worse since they were dating. Then she'd felt protected and complimented. Now that they were living together, he wanted to know where she was every minute. She felt suffocated.

When tears threatened again, she shook herself mentally. She didn't have time for this now. She'd been away too long. She repaired her mascara, inspected her face in the mirror and decided her color was almost normal. She hoped Lisa had been successful and Annette wouldn't have noticed how long she'd been gone.

To the Reader

Discovering Your Buddha Nature

Nancy is trying to understand and handle a complex situation with Doug, but she's confused and scared. We all face problems like this in our lives, where we don't seem to have the clarity or wisdom to handle them. You might be exhausted by such a situation yourself.

Sometimes we are just too tired to summon up the energy to face it, so the problem continues unresolved. It could be that we've learned life patterns which don't allow us to recognize what is in front of us, or prevent us from taking action. Or it could be we haven't encountered what we need to know in our life experience to resolve the situation.

When we encounter a situation such as this, we appear to be deadlocked.

Buddhism teaches that when each of us is functioning according to our birthright, there is no problem which cannot be resolved. Deep within, you have unlimited power, a higher level of wisdom, unshakeable happiness and freedom. This is called your Buddha Nature.

When you learn to access it, you will be able to surmount any deadlock and your individuality will blossom. Later in the book you will learn the practice which will allow you to do this.

When you tap into your Buddha nature on a daily basis, your life will begin to turn in the direction of creating personal happiness and value. Even if your life has been immersed in negativity, pulled toward misfortune and un-happiness, it too will be redirected and pulled in the op-posite direction, toward happiness.

One of the great joys of introducing someone to the practice is to watch that great redirection happen. An-other is seeing a unique individuality gradually unfold and blossom.

You were born to live an absolutely, happy life, true to yourself, making your unique contribution to the world. Although it seems unlikely now, you will learn you are a Buddha.

3

Oneness of Self and Environment

When Nancy arrived breathless at the front office, Annette fortunately was nowhere to be seen. She glanced over the counter to the waiting room. Good, no one there. She started to adjust the yellow and blue iris sitting in the vase on the counter. This was the agency's one concession to beauty. She wished they'd paint the walls in something other than beige. A drab waiting room couldn't feel welcoming to the clients. She gave the flowers a final touch, just in time to pick up the phone when it rang. "Family Service, this is Nancy, may I help you?"

The male voice on the other end of the line sounded shaky. "I need to see someone. I'm having a lot of trouble with panic attacks. I feel like I can't breathe." The voice started to rise.

"You're going to be all right," Nancy said. "We are here to help you." She knew she had to project calmness, to settle down the man listening.

"You'll need to come to our office. Do you know where we are? "

"I looked it up before I called you," said the uncertain voice.

"How would you get here?" She tried to keep him focused.

"I don't know. Having to go outside to the bus, well that's really hard. I haven't been able to leave the house for months."

He won't be able to leave the house to come to us either.

Aloud she said, "Have you ever heard of Treetops, the streetside mental health group? If you can't get here, they could come and pick you up in their van. They would have a therapist with them."

"I think I could do it, if I didn't have to come by myself."

"Here is their number," said Nancy. "Call me back when you've talked to them." She could keep him company on the phone while he waited.

She became aware of someone watching her and turned. She recognized Sue, the head of the social work department. "You're doing fine Nancy," said Sue, smiling. "You handled him well."

Sue was entirely different from Annette, thought Nancy. She was easy going and didn't try to control the people working for her. She felt she could relax with Sue, not have to be on her guard as she was with Annette.

"Thanks," said Nancy. The phone rang again.

The shaky voice. "I did it and they're coming."

"Good," said Nancy. "Tell me a little about yourself while we wait." She settled in to listen. About five minutes later he responded to a knock on his door. "They're here now."

"You can do it. I'll look forward to meeting you when you get here," said Nancy. She turned around but Sue had left.

This was the part of the job she liked, the contact with the clients. She wished she could supervise the front office and train the other staff how to handle clients. Sometimes they were too abrupt and hurried.

She could enter data into the computer, file and set up charts in her sleep. She looked around her work space. She'd like to reorganize it to smooth out the work flow and redecorate to make the area more welcoming to clients. Her management experience had given her an eye for what needed to be done.

This wasn't a bad job, but the pay was low. She wished she could have afforded to search longer for a job.

The door to the waiting room opened and a panicky-looking man walked in, followed by a man with a Treetops logo on his shirt.

"You must be the person I talked to on the phone," said Nancy.

His eyes warmed. "You were a great help to me," he responded. "I was able to get here."

"I'm glad I was able to be of help."

She picked up the phone. "Annette, this is Nancy. We have a client who just arrived who's having a panic attack and will need a therapist right away."

"I'll take it from here," said Annette.

Lisa walked casually into the front office. Nancy beckoned her over. "How did you keep Annette away?" asked Nancy in a low voice.

"I asked her a question about how to set up the training DVDs in the library," Lisa whispered.

Warmth stole over Nancy. Lisa was a good friend. She'd taken a risk to help her. "I really appreciate your running interference for me."

Lisa smiled at her. "You've done it for me."

Clients came and went all day. By three in the afternoon, Nancy felt bone tired. She glanced at the clock. She still had two hours to go. Weariness washed over her. Why had she been so tired recently?

She envied Lisa, who seemed full of energy. She looked happier too. She hadn't called Nancy aside to discuss problems for a month or so. Nancy wondered about that. Their relationship had developed through extended discussions regarding personal issues, and Lisa had always had plenty to contribute.

Lately, Nancy was the one with the problems and Lisa had been giving her support but not bringing up any of her own. Lisa must be doing better in her life. She'd have to ask her. But not now; she was too tired to do anything but just get through the rest of the day. She settled in to finish the new files.

To the Reader

You Are One With Your Environment

Nancy is working in an agency which, in some ways, is a negative experience for her. Her supervisor, Annette, is making life difficult and Nancy doesn't make enough money to live on.

There are some positive aspects to Nancy's workplace as well. She works in a situation where she can demonstrate and use the positive side of her nature, which responds to people who are struggling. Sue and Lisa are supportive, positive influences around her.

What about you? Is there an area of your life where you feel you are helpless? Maybe you, like Nancy, haven't yet realized that you have the power to recreate your circumstances and make them more to your liking.

Most people see their environment as something that was established and existed prior to their arrival. They were born into it and believe they were born by chance into whatever life circumstances existed at their birth. Whether they were fortunate or unfortunate, they're taught these circumstances had nothing to do with them.

That way of thinking persists into how they view their lives. They see themselves as entering a work environment which is separate from them. If there are problems at work, they probably think of the problem as lying with the company or with another individual. If they are having financial problems, they see the issues as belonging to a weak economy, or to having no jobs in a small town.

Buddhism would say that the environment reflects the people living in it. Have you had the experience of going to a house where a happy family lived? Were you enveloped by a warm feeling as you entered the front door? Conversely, you may have visited the home of someone who has suffered from depression, who has neglected his personal appearance. Maybe dust sat on the tables. Overall, you didn't feel welcomed.

Buddhism would take this concept further. Everything in your experience, including work, the people you know, and the quality of your relationships, is a reflection of your inner life. Although you may perceive things as separate, there is a dimension of your life that is one with the universe. Through that connection, you manifest all the circumstances of your life in the objective world.

Nichiren Daishonin would say, "There are not two lands, pure or impure in themselves. The difference lies solely in the good or evil of our minds." Evil in this case refers to actions based on greed, aggression, fear, or anger.

Practioners have seen this principle demonstrated clearly time and again. One woman related the story of a house on her street. An attractive family home sat on a nice lot two houses down the street from her. Then the owner became involved with the drug world, and the house morphed into a weedy, unkempt, garbage-strewn environment that repelled every on-looker. The people who lived there were the same people as before, but the state of their minds had totally changed. Their home environment reflected that change.

Practitioners have been asked, "You mean you're blaming people for their situation?" Buddhism doesn't assign blame. Your situation is the outworking of the law of cause and effect, which will be discussed in a later chapter. For now it is enough to know that because you have the power to create a situation, you also have the power to change it.

The Ten Worlds: the Lower Six

That evening after work, Nancy climbed the stairs to their second floor apartment. All she wanted to do was close her eyes and rest. That might not happen, though, with Doug drinking so much. In the beginning, their apartment, with its view over the park, had felt like a sanctuary. Now, it felt more like a potential minefield.

But in spite of everything, she was glad to be home. Doug was sitting in the navy blue lounger with his feet up, watching TV. That TV had been the cause of one of their arguments. They didn't have the money but he'd insisted upon putting it on credit anyway.

He held a drink. Her heart sank. She'd hoped he'd be in a good humor tonight. She was too tired to deal with a drunk.

Doug got up and hugged her.

"Ow," Nancy flinched slightly. Her breasts felt tender against his chest.

"You're later than usual. How come?"

Uh-oh, here came Doug's inquisition. Dread clutched her stomach. "We worked late. We had more clients than usual today."

His eyebrows rose. "This late? It's after six-thirty. Where did you go after work?"

"I told you," Nancy said, trying not to sound annoyed. "We just finished getting off work."

Doug flashed a disbelieving look. "Give me a break! Listen. I don't like it when you go off and do things without me after work. This is supposed to be our time."

Nancy sighed. *Here he goes again.* These days he wanted her with him all the time when he was home. Since he'd lost that account at work, he'd withdrawn from their friends. Now it was just the two of them.

Nancy rubbed her temples wearily. "If you don't believe me, I don't know what else to say," she said. "That's the truth." Sometimes she wondered why she stayed.

She headed for the kitchen to start dinner. She wouldn't get to rest after all. Why couldn't he cook dinner sometimes? After all, they both worked.

He followed her to the kitchen. "I miss you when you aren't here."

"I know," she said hoping to placate him. "I miss you too." Agreeing with him often settled him down. If she tried to defend herself or resisted him in any way then he would escalate. It just wasn't worth it when he'd been drinking.

It worked this time. Apparently satisfied, he went back to the living room. Shortly she heard the voice of the newscaster.

While she cut red and green pepper strips for the stir fry, she reflected on how much their life had changed. At the beginning, she'd looked forward to being with him. The intimacy of living with someone had taken her breath away. She'd loved touching him in the mornings before he awakened, feeling his silky skin in the tender places, watching him sleep. He was so male—his coarse curly brown hair and toned muscles had such a wonderful texture. She'd inhale the smell of his skin. Her life had been full of wonder and new discoveries, the ecstasies of sex and the fulfillment of establishing a life with him.

Doug walked back into the kitchen. He placed his glass under the ice dispenser.

Nancy couldn't resist saying, "I wish you wouldn't drink any more before dinner." He ignored her, frowning, as cubes fell into the glass. She wished she could keep her mouth shut. But his drinking worried her.

Lately, there'd been other changes in his personality. He was more impatient and angry. Last weekend, when he had more to drink than usual, he scared her. The next morning, he couldn't seem to remember what had happened the evening before.

Doug took a sip of his drink. "Hey, Babe, why don't we go to a movie tonight," he said. "We haven't gone out for a while."

Weariness flooded over her. She wished he'd leave her alone. "I think I'm too tired to do anything tonight," she said. "I want to go to bed right after dinner." She cranked the pepper mill over the stir fry and then picked up a wooden spoon to turn it.

"What's the matter with you?" yelled Doug.

She startled and nearly dropped the spoon.

With a clank, he set down his tumbler. "You never want to go out or have fun anymore!"

Surprised by his observation, she put him off. "Maybe Friday night, when I don't have to work late?" He was right.

She remembered the soreness of her breasts when he hugged her. All at once she was fully alert, the tiredness gone completely, adrenalin coursing through her. What time of the month was it? She couldn't remember. She searched the wall calendar frantically.

Doug persisted. "Why not tonight? Friday is two days away."

"I said, I'm too tired," Nancy repeated. How long since her last period? She stared at the calendar. A sinking feeling enveloped her as she realized it was six weeks ago.

It can't be! I can't be pregnant! Not now, not with my relationship with Doug on the rocks.

Maybe she was seeing things that weren't there, she thought with desperation. Deep down she knew that wasn't true. There was only one other time she had experienced this kind of tiredness, during her first pregnancy at sixteen. She never told Doug that she'd had a baby and placed her for adoption. She wondered how he would take that news. She shook herself mentally. She couldn't worry about that right now.

First thing in the morning she'd call for an appointment with a gynecologist. She had to know for sure and she didn't trust the pregnancy tests to be accurate. This could change everything.

She dreaded having to ask Annette for the time off for the visit to the doctor. She wasn't going to like it if Nancy asked for more time out of the office.

Doug ambled over and put his arms around her neck. "Is dinner about ready?" He nuzzled her hair. She could smell the alcohol on his breath and a faint unease filled her.

"Just about," she said. Briefly she leaned against him. Her emotions roiled in a swirl. Elation, fear, happiness, and panic chased through her. Maybe he'd drunk too much to notice. Now she wondered instead of being too tired, if she would be able to sleep at all.

To the Reader

Identifying Internal States

In this last chapter we have seen Nancy and Doug having problems in their relationship. Maybe you have had a relationship problem of your own.

Buddhism would say that everyone has ten internal states, or ten worlds, that we live internally every day in response to outside stimuli. Let's discuss the six lower ones, as this is where Nancy and Doug are currently living in their relationship.

The six lower worlds are as follows:

Hell – (stuck, miserable)

Hunger – (unfulfilled cravings)

Animality – (law of the jungle)

Anger – (arrogance, jealousy)

Humanity – (neutral, calm)

Rapture – (temporary or relative happiness)

The lower worlds are reactive to circumstances. To show you how they work, let's look at a typical day in anyone's life. You get up and read the newspaper and see a politician has done something that makes you angry. You are in the world of anger. You go to the office and your boss says you will earn a trip to Hawaii if you sell so many widgets. For a moment, you are in the world of hunger. Your significant other calls, and you move into the world of rapture. He or she tells you they want to end your relationship. You fall into hell.

Doug is living in the world of hunger with his drinking, and unfulfilled cravings. He shifts easily into the world of anger. Nancy tries to stay in the world of humanity but readily falls into hell, feeling stuck and miserable.

The lower worlds lead to suffering. You might easily see why the four lowest worlds could lead to suffering. But, the worlds of rapture and humanity? Yes, even the worlds of rapture and humanity eventually lead to suffering.

Rapture represents the world of gratification. You achieve some desire. Even though you will be happy for a short while, these desires lead to temporary happiness and then the rapture is gone. A person in the world of humanity is quite vulnerable to falling into the lower worlds. I'm sure you have all known someone who seems calm and then, when faced with some bad news, readily falls apart.

If you read the morning papers, you've seen person after person suffer because of being lost in one of the lower worlds. For example, you read about assaults, child abuse, and domestic violence, due to someone living in the world of anger. When many people fall into one of the four lower worlds, society as a whole suffers as well. For example, you've undoubtedly read many stories about a group of investment firms who have let the world of hunger or greed dominate their business, causing suffering for many people.

Later on in the book we will discuss the four higher worlds and you will be introduced to a pathway leading out of suffering. The good news is that we are not condemned to suffering. On the contrary, it is our birthright to be happy.

5

Adverse Circumstances Can Lead to Growth

The next morning, Nancy left a voicemail for Annette saying she wouldn't be in because of a doctor's appointment. She felt like a coward, but she just couldn't deal with Annette right now.

Feeling tense, she opened the door to the gynecologist's office. As she sat filling out forms, she hoped that she was wrong. Maybe she was only a little late. She clung to the hope that she could go on with normal life. A nurse called her into the doctor's office.

Shortly, Dr. Martin strode in and greeted her with a firm handshake. She looked to be in her forties and there was a no nonsense air to her which Nancy liked. "So you think you're pregnant?"

Nancy nodded. Dr. Martin picked up a pen and made a note. She looked up. "Is this your first pregnancy?" Nancy flushed. She knew she'd be asked this question but it always hurt to answer it.

"No, I had a little girl when I was sixteen. My family didn't want to raise her. They wanted me to finish school, so I had to place her for adoption."

The doctor's face softened. "That must have been hard."

"Very." Nancy looked away. "It still is. I wonder about her all the time."

The doctor asked a number of questions about her health, whether there had been any issues with her first pregnancy, and how far along she thought she was. Then the nurse took Nancy into the exam room. The doctor came in, snapping on rubber gloves. The exam always made her feel uncomfortable, but Nancy submitted.

As the doctor took measurements, she said to Nancy, "I think you're six or so weeks pregnant. When did you have your last period?"

"Six weeks is right," Nancy said, trying to keep her voice from quavering. "I had circled it on the calendar." She closed her eyes briefly, taking it all in.

The confirmed pregnancy made her feel felt both excited and despondent. Now there was no doubt. She didn't know what to do about telling Doug. Then there was work. What would Annette do when she found out? Anxiety bloomed until she reminded herself that she didn't have to tell anyone, for a while.

Finally, she was released by the doctor's office. She just had to tell someone her news. When she got home, Nancy called her sister Sara and the two agreed to meet in the park.

Sara's family and their mother had moved from the Midwest to Eugene in 1985. Initially Nancy had debated staying in Cincinnati, but the pull of being near her sister was too strong and in 1997 she'd moved to Oregon too.

At the park, Nancy waited for Sara, watching the Willamette river flow by. Water rippling over the rocks soothed her. Beyond the river, cars motored on the expressway. Her tension eased. Out of the office on a work day and not sick either, she felt as though she'd dropped out of workday life.

Dark curls bouncing, Sara almost ran onto the path. She had a habit of usually being late and was in a habitual hurry. She hugged Nancy and held her shoulders to look at her. "You look tired." She looked trim as always, wearing a leather jacket, with jeans and polished black boots.

"I've been tired." For a moment she debated whether she should tell her sister, then couldn't stand the idea of being alone with her news. Reluctantly she said, "I just found out for sure I'm pregnant."

"That's wonderful!" Sara's brown eyes opened wide and a delighted grin split her face. She hugged Nancy again. *She could say that*. Sara had Troy, a husband who adored her and they were happy together. It was so different with her and Doug.

"It's not a very good time for me to be pregnant," Nancy said. "Doug and I haven't been getting along. This couldn't have come at a worse time."

Sara's delighted look sobered into concern. "How do you think he'll take the news?"

Nancy hesitated, looking out over the calming river to help her stay focused. "I'm not sure I'm going to tell him until I see what happens with the relationship." This was the first time Nancy had really acknowledged this to herself.

"Don't you think he has the right to know?" asked Sara.

"Yes, but I have to decide what I'm going to do before I tell him." Nancy hadn't planned to tell Sara what was going on at home, but the pressure built until she blurted it out. "He's been drinking too much. He changes when he drinks and scares me. He has a temper now. Frankly, I worry what he'd be like around a young child. And he's so possessive I can't breathe."

"Oh dear, I see what you mean by a bad time. Have you told Mom?"

Nancy shook her head. "I know what Mom would want me to do. She'd want me to stay no matter what." She pictured her traditional mother goading her into staying with Doug for the child's sake. She swept that thought out of her mind.

"She probably would," Sara said.

"You *know* she would," Nancy said. "I can't tell her until I'm ready. Promise you won't either."

"I promise," Sara said. When Nancy had been pregnant before, Sara had been a support to her while the family was trying to decide what to do. Five years older, Sara had felt as badly as Nancy when the decision was made to place her baby.

Sara looked directly into Nancy's eyes. "Are you thinking about leaving Doug?"

Hearing the words shocked Nancy. "I hadn't put it into so many words." She held her head with her hands. "I just need a little more time to sort everything out."

"Boy, you're dealing with a lot." Sara patted Nancy's shoulder. "But don't forget. We're always here if you need us."

"I know," Nancy said, giving her sister a squeeze. It was wonderful having Sara in town, but Mom? *That* she wasn't so sure about. As Sara and Nancy walked out of the park and back to their cars, Nancy tried not to worry. She'd deal with her mother, and Doug, later.

The next morning when Nancy arrived at work, Lisa gave her an inquiring look. "I'll talk to you later," Nancy mouthed. Lisa nodded.

At noon, Nancy couldn't hold the news to herself any longer. She went over to Lisa's desk. "Lunch?"

"I'd love to," Lisa said. "Applebee's?" She turned off her computer, grabbed her jacket and they headed for the front door.

Over the sounds of the other diners talking, sipping her ice tea, Lisa looked curious. "What was going on this morning when you came in to work? You looked as though you'd seen a ghost."

"Was it that obvious?" asked Nancy. Lisa nodded.

Nancy took a deep breath and plunged in. "I found out yesterday I'm pregnant. I guess I'm in shock."

"Really?" breathed Lisa. Nancy could imagine her coworker assessing all the ramifications.

"How does Doug feel about it?"

"I haven't told him."

Lisa raised her eyebrows.

The waitress interrupted. "Ready to order?" They both turned.

"I'll have chicken salad," said Nancy.

"Make that two," said Lisa. The waitressed scribbled the orders on her pad and turned away. Lisa leaned across the table. "So. How far along do you think you are?"

Nancy stared at the salt shaker. "About six weeks."

"So you have some time before you'll show."

"I'm glad I found out early," said Nancy. "I'll have time to decide what to do." Across the aisle, the waitresses were singing happy birthday to a customer sitting in front of a chocolate cupcake with a candle burning on it. *I hope it will be a happy birthday for this baby.*

After participating in the singing, their waitress broke away from the group and then appeared at the end of their table with their chicken salads. She poured two more ice teas.

The waitress moved to another table and Lisa quietly asked, "Do you want this baby?"

Nancy felt shocked. Of course she did. She had wanted a baby ever since she had placed the last one for adoption. She still thought of her, wondered what she looked like and if she was happy. She couldn't lose a second child. "Oh, yes," she said. "I've wanted a baby for a long time. I'm just confused about Doug, the way things are right now."

"Lots to think about," Lisa said cheerfully.

Why was she always so positive lately?

They turned to their salads. Nancy couldn't stop thinking about how Lisa's attitude had changed. Recently, it seemed as if nothing fazed her. She possessed peacefulness, a serenity that piqued Nancy's curiosity.

Over coffee, Nancy drew up her courage. "I've been wondering if I've been imagining things. You don't seem to have so many problems lately and you act happier."

Lisa grinned. "I *am* happier. Remember the chanting I told you about?"

Nancy nodded.

Lisa went on. "I've been doing exactly what the more experienced people at the Buddhist center have told me to do and my life is working much better." She paused, as if debating whether to say more. Then she added, "Yours could too."

"You really think so?" Nancy asked. "Even with the pregnancy and everything?"

Lisa nodded. "I'm sure of it. You should come with me to a meeting and hear the experiences of the other people," she said. "I'm still new. They can explain it better than I can." She pulled out her calendar. "There's a meeting tomorrow, if you'd like to come."

Nancy weighed the offer. Her life certainly wasn't going very well and Lisa had changed. She was noticeably happier. Her frown lines were gone and she had more serenity in her face. She didn't talk about problems anymore. That was a big difference.

If anyone needed something to change, Nancy did. That was for sure. It would be a hassle dealing with Doug, if she decided to go to the meeting. She could already hear the arguments.

"When's the meeting? Daytime or evening?"

"Evening, why?"

She shrugged. "Oh nothing. It's just harder for me to do things in the evenings. That's when Doug wants me home." She couldn't keep going as she had been, and crazy as it sounded, this chanting thing seemed to have made a difference for Lisa. Briefly she debated back and forth and then came to a decision. "Maybe I'll come after all," she said.

A pleased look crossed Lisa's face. "I'll pick you up at six-thirty."

"Just honk. Don't come up. It'll be easier for me to get away." Nancy could hardly believe she'd said such a thing. How had things gotten to this point?

Lisa frowned. "It's that hard?"

"You have no idea. That's why I'm coming. Something's got to change."

36

She might regret it when she told Doug, but she had to do something to make her life work better. She had the baby to think about now.

To The Reader

Using Obstacles to Grow

Nancy, challenged by her circumstances, has begun searching for a better way. She has admitted to herself she doesn't know what to do and has taken the first step toward trying to improve her life. She trusts Lisa, even though she still thinks the idea of chanting to improve her life sounds rather odd.

At this point she has no idea of what she will encounter, but she is open. As long as you think you know how things work, you may not be open to change. Sometimes challenging circumstances force you to try something new.

President Ikeda is the head of this Buddhist organization, the SGI, (Soka Gakkai International.) He is the author of sixty books, has received 250 awards, and has been a humanistic leader for fifty years.

He says how we react at the darkest of times determines the course of our lives. We have the choice whether to revert to our negative nature, or to embrace our positive side. If we see everything in only a negative or pessimistic light, then our lives will gradually be taken over by darkness. On the other hand, if we regard everything that happens as something to create future happiness and value, no matter how our current circumstances look on the surface, then our lives will take an upward turn.

Nancy, because of her adverse circumstances, has made the choice to look into something new. By agreeing to go to the meeting, she has taken the first step to changing her life.

6

Relative Versus Unshakeable Happiness

The next evening, Nancy came home exhausted as usual. It was meeting night, and she was excited to learn more about the practice. She sighed. She'd have to tell Doug she was going out. She braced herself for the barrage of questions that were sure to follow.

He'd already started drinking. She gathered her courage and gave him a brief kiss. "I want to get dinner on the table," she said casually. "I'm going to a meeting tonight."

Doug had looked pleased to see her, but now he frowned. "Where are you going?

"I want to investigate something which looks interesting."

"I want you to spend time with me." He looked imploring, his gaze holding hers. "Is it too much to ask? When I come home from work, I want you home."

Guilt flashed through Nancy. *Maybe I am being unreasonable.* She felt a pang in her heart. "I know you want me here, but sometimes I need time to do something for myself."

"I wish you'd think of how I feel." He looked tired and rumpled.

Nancy did think of how he felt, but she didn't think he returned the concern. It wouldn't do any good to argue though. She just hoped she could pacify him, so she could slip out when Lisa pulled up out front. She'd never done anything like this before, but she was just too tired to have a confrontation.

"Why don't I put some dinner together? Is there something you would particularly like?"

Doug smiled. "How about pizza?"

"Coming right up." She went into the kitchen to prepare it for him. By this time in the day she had lost most of her energy. It was silly, but she felt guilty about going anywhere when he wanted her at home. She hoped this meeting would be worth the trouble.

Just as she set the pizza in front of Doug, a horn beeped outside. Lisa, she thought, anxiety spiking. Doug was busy with his first bite.

"Aren't you going to sit down with me?" he asked. Nancy could tell he was sure he had won.

"Not tonight," she replied. "I told you I was going out." She ran down the stairs. As she climbed into the car, she glanced up. Doug stood in front of the window, frowning and staring down at her. She could see he was upset.

"That's Doug?" Lisa asked.

Nancy nodded.

"He doesn't look very happy."

"He's not," Nancy said. "He doesn't like it when I go out without him. This is part of the problem. He's gotten possessive and sometimes I feel I can't breathe."

Lisa raised her eyebrows in a question mark.

Nancy added quickly, "Let's not talk about it now."

Lisa shrugged and turned her attention to driving.

♦

Doug watched the car turn the corner and turned away from the window. He couldn't believe what had just happened. Nancy had never just left him and gone off by herself before.

"What's she so excited about," he muttered. A sense of foreboding crept over him. Everything had been going so well. Nancy had been what he wanted in a woman, a quiet unassuming person who let him be the leader in the household. Usually she abided by what he wanted. Now this.

He opened a bag of potato chips and plopped down in front of the TV set. He missed having Nancy with him. They usually watched TV together in the evenings. Their favorite show would be on in about five minutes.

He decided to open that new bottle of wine. Nancy wasn't around to tell him he shouldn't do it. He got out of the recliner and headed for the kitchen.

Five minutes later, settled back in the recliner with his drink. By eight o'clock he felt buzzed. But he was still thinking about Nancy.

Where *was* she anyway? She should have been back by now. And who was that woman she was with? Not anyone he knew, he was sure. He was tempted to call her, but then remembered he didn't know where she was and she'd left her cell phone on the table. Frustrated he poured another glass of wine. If she was out having fun, he could have fun too.

He surfed the stations again and obsessed about what he'd say when Nancy came in. He was starting to get angry. What if she had gone to meet another man?

To the Reader

Happiness Grows From the Inside Out

Doug is basing his happiness on one thing after another outside of himself. He relies on Nancy to make him happy. He thinks drinking or watching TV makes him happy. He believes he is happy on a sunny day and depressed on a rainy day, as if the weather makes a difference to his happiness.

He doesn't recognize that basing his happiness on any of these things, including the satisfaction of all desires, means that he is counting on things and people, which are temporary and always subject to change. He is looking for what every person wants: a source of happiness which isn't going to be temporary, but which will be lasting. Do you know anyone who isn't looking for that?

Think about the world you live in. Doesn't everything change over time? This includes the physical things which seem long-lived, people, buildings, etc. Joy deriving from getting something you desire may seem quite genuine and it is—for a while. Eventually, though, even this kind of joy gives way to restlessness and dissatisfaction. Buddhism calls this *relative happiness.*

Doug hasn't learned that no one else, even a lover, can make him fundamentally happy. A lover can bring us some degree of happiness, but the large number of divorces in the US testifies to the fact that finding happiness in this way is not the ultimate answer.

Buddhism would say that happiness always grows from the inside out. Each person must achieve it for oneself. True happiness is achieved by developing our character and capacities to fully realize our potential. A lover is icing on the cake.

Buddhism teaches that the source of absolute happiness lies deep within each of us. You were introduced to that source. It is called the Buddha nature, the highest level of human life.

Doug is searching everywhere else but inside himself. When Doug learns that he can find the greatest source of happiness inside of himself, then he too will be able to start walking the path to becoming truly happy.

"Happiness is not something that someone else, like a lover, can give to us. True happiness is obtained through fully realizing our potential."
Daisaku Ikeda, *Faith into Action.* p. 36

Introduction to Buddhist Practice

As Lisa and Nancy opened the door to the community center, Nancy saw an unpretentious space decorated in green and gold. The artwork on the walls was probably done by the members. She could hear the sound of people chanting but couldn't see them.

They walked over to the front desk. The man sitting there looked up and smiled. "May I help you?"

Lisa gestured to Nancy. "This is the first time Nancy's been here and I'd like someone to help me explain Buddhism to her. I'm pretty new myself."

Nancy stole a peek into the other room. The chanting piqued her curiosity.

The man nodded. "I'll find someone to talk with you." He beckoned to a white-haired woman standing in an adjoining larger room.

She came over and extended her hand to each of them. "I'm Vicky." She had a nice firm handshake. No wimp here, Nancy thought.

Vicky gestured to the bigger room. "Why don't you come in and I'll explain what's going on."

As Nancy followed Vicky through the doorway, the chanting became louder. About twenty people all faced the front of the room. They came from all walks of life:

Japanese, Latino, Caucasian, and African-American. Their eyes were focused on a large gold scroll covered in Chinese characters, written in black calligraphy. The scroll hung in a beautifully finished wooden housing, doors folded back to the sides, illuminated by both light inside the housing and from the front. The light made the scroll almost glow. Nancy had never seen anything so beautiful.

The people chanting held their hands together in the prayer position, beads loosely looped through the fingers of both hands and crossed once in the middle. One person sat in front of the others chanting into a microphone. Nancy understood quickly that his louder voice kept the group chanting together.

"What do you know about Buddhism?" Vicky asked.

Lisa answered. "I'm still new and Nancy doesn't know anything, except that I think it's helping me."

Nancy responded. "I did a meditation practice for a while, but it was an inward practice."

Vicky nodded. "As you can see, this is an outward chanting practice. It will be different for you."

She pointed to the scroll. "The scroll is called a Gohonzon and it hangs inside a Butsudan. It represents all the possible states of life a person lives internally every day. It acts as a mirror for each person to reflect on his or her life. The large letters down the center are Nam-myoho-renge-kyo, which represent our Buddha nature, the highest level of life."

"So, people are praying to the Gohonzon?" Nancy was a bit confused.

Vicky shook her head. "No. The practitioners are not praying to a God outside of themselves. That would go against the essential belief in Buddhism, which is that universal life force and wisdom reside *inside* each of us, in our Buddha nature."

Lisa turned to Vicky. "I haven't taught her the chant yet."

Vicky smiled. "Good time to begin. We're about to do *gongyo* which includes chanting Nam-myo-ho-renge-kyo and reciting two books of the Lotus Sutra, which Shakamuni taught 2500 years ago and said was his highest teaching. I'll show you what to do." She opened a book, which looked as though it was written in Chinese.

"*Gongyo* takes about fifteen minutes and then we'll have a meeting until eight-thirty to introduce people to Buddhism. You can hear experiences, learn something about the philosophy, and ask questions."

Nancy said, "That's what I hoped for."

They sat down on comfortable chairs facing the Gohonzon and Vicky pointed to the first line in the book. The leader tapped the bell three times.

"What's the language?" Nancy felt nervous.

Vicky said, "Ancient Chinese."

"That looks hard."

"It takes a while to learn, but before long you're chanting it as though it was second nature."

The leader began. "Nam-myo-renge-kyo."

Even as Nancy struggled to follow Vicky's finger pointing out the words, she recognized that the recitation was really lovely. It had a rhythmical nature. There was a lively, yet peaceful, energy in the room.

After a few minutes, she just relaxed and listened. The sadness, which had enveloped her since leaving home, dissipated like smoke. When the group chanted Nam-myoho-renge-kyo for five minutes, she joined in and felt herself becoming more peaceful, connected to something larger than herself.

Prayers followed. The one she liked best was the prayer for people who had died. She thought of her father who had died a couple of years before, and her heart went out to him.

A feeling of comfort came over her. She could pray for him every day.

When *gongyo* ended, Nancy felt peaceful, energized and connected.

Vicky encouraged Nancy and Lisa to sit at a table in the back of the room. A few others joined them.

A man who introduced himself as Scott started the discussion. "Could everyone introduce themselves and how long you've practiced?" He turned to a man next to him. "Hi Bill. Good to see you back."

Bill, a tall lanky man, smiled.

Nancy took a deep breath. "I'm Nancy and this is the first time I've been to a meeting." She soon learned that she was the newest person there. Of the others, Bill had practiced for a month, Lisa for two. Suzanne, who looked Middle Eastern, had practiced for fifteen years. Vicky and Scott had each practiced for twenty-five. Hanako, a small Japanese woman, had been chanting the longest, forty-three years. Nancy wondered what it was about this practice that someone would keep at it for so long.

Scott asked, "Does anyone have any questions or an experience to share?"

Bill leaned forward, hesitantly speaking up, brushing his bangs out of his face. "I've been chanting for a month. You told me to set a goal and so I did and I've been chanting about ten minutes a day for it."

Bill looked as though life had been hard recently. He looked tense and a little scruffy, his clothes worn.

Scott asked, "Have you noticed anything change in your life?"

"I'm not sure. You remember I have my own hairdressing business? With the change in the economy things are going downhill. I set a goal to find a buyer for my business and then find a job. Right now I have an interested buyer, and also have someone interested in hiring me. But nothing has actually happened yet."

"Don't be discouraged," Scott responded. "You've taken two big steps forward. You have a person interested in your business and another in hiring you. That's real progress."

He gave Bill a smile of encouragement. "It's important to remember that you move step by step toward a goal. Noticing those steps of progress keeps you encouraged."

Hanako's eyes sparkled as she spoke. "Just make sure you keep praying and chanting until you get your goal. Don't stop now. Always keep chanting until you achieve your goal."

Nancy frowned. "I never heard of chanting for practical goals before. That doesn't seem very spiritual to me."

Scott responded. "When you chant, you are activating the Buddha nature within, that part of you which is connected with everything. When you achieve one goal after another, your faith will grow, as will your awareness that you are one with all things. You'll become happy."

Hanako leaned forward. "Nichiren Daishonin, the founder of the practice, used to say that when you're evaluating whether a religion is right for you, you should know that the people who are doing it achieve actual results in life. If you don't have that, what's the point?"

Hmm, Nancy thought. She'd never heard of a religion which expected you to have proof. How provocative. Nancy asked, "I've wanted to move up the ladder in my job, but I'm afraid to ask for additional responsibilities. How should I chant for a goal like that?"

Vicky smiled. "Set your goal. Be specific about what you want to have happen. Then chant for it."

"I'm afraid to say anything. I have a supervisor who doesn't like me very well."

Vicky gazed at Nancy with kind, warm eyes. "That happened to me too. I had fears of doing the things I had to do to achieve my goal. When you set a goal and then come up against something in yourself that stops you, then you chant to have the courage to step through that fear."

Vicky straightened her back and looked at the new people for emphasis. "When you do take the action, you'll become stronger. This is your first step toward enlightenment. Negativity, in this case your fear, is what we call fundamental darkness. We all have it. It obscures the fact that we have the capacity to create our lives exactly the way we want them."

Nancy looked at Vicky. "What'd you do to get through the fear?"

"I chanted longer for courage and confidence. I had to spend a half an hour to an hour a day chanting, because I was always stopped by my fear. One day, after chanting, I wasn't afraid. I just walked right in—before I lost my confidence—and asked my boss to give me more responsibility. The funny thing is that it turned out there was no reason to be afraid. My boss was very pleased that I'd come in and asked."

Nancy nodded. "Hmm." She didn't know if she could do this or not.

Bill said, "I have to get out so early in the morning that I find myself chanting in the car and I don't have time to learn *gongyo*."

Again, Hanako was encouraging. "It takes time to establish a new habit. Even if you only chant five minutes, you're moving forward and will get benefit. Just keep at it." Bill nodded.

Vicky added, "I know that some people get their clothes and lunch ready the night before, just to give that little extra time in the morning."

Nancy asked, "Could you all tell me why you chant?"

Suzanne was in her fifties, with dark eyes, fair skin and a curly black mane which cascaded below her shoulders. "A few years ago, my husband unexpectedly told me he was going to divorce me. I'd grown up in a family with major financial problems and had a core fear of being put on the street. I'd never been successful in holding a full-time job and I needed a hip replacement too. I absolutely panicked."

"I can see why," Bill said.

"I called a friend and told her what had happened and said I didn't know what to do." Suzanne paused. "My friend said, 'I don't know what you should do either, but this is what I would do.' She taught me to chant Nam-myoho-renge-kyo."

Scott commented. "Each person has a different experience, don't they?" Heads nodded around the room.

Suzanne continued. "The next year was absolutely amazing. I chanted every day. I ended up with a little house that was all paid for. I had enough money for basic expenses. My ex's insurance paid for the hip replacement."

Bill looked incredulous. "Amazing." He seemed to hang on her every word.

Suzanne smiled. "I found a job as an on-line teacher, which used my training as a special-ed teacher. Then I was able to move out of a small town, which didn't have many job opportunities." She took a deep breath. "I wouldn't dare not chant every day," she concluded.

Boy, thought Nancy. That's pretty wild. But how did she connect her circumstances with chanting? Those things might have happened anyway.

Hanako spoke up. "Suzanne's story brings up an important point. When you chant for something, you never have any idea of how it's going to work out. You just chant with your completed goal in mind, and let the universe work out the path to reach it. That's a real change from what we are taught, which is to strategize about it first. But you can see that there was no way Suzanne could have known what was going to happen."

Nancy felt skeptical. "How do you know there's even a connection between the chanting and Suzanne's results? I don't see it."

Vicky answered. "We know because we've each done our own experiment. I'm going to suggest you try it. Pick a goal that would be a stretch, something that you think is out of reach. Then chant for it for ninety days and see what happens."

Scott turned to Nancy. "You're going to find that when you chant Nam-myoho-renge-kyo and take action toward your goal, you'll be able to overcome things which have blocked you." A couple of practitioners nodded and murmured agreement.

He gave Nancy a warm smile. "I know it's hard to believe. You'll just have to test it out for yourself. This is an experiential practice."

Nancy remembered the fight she had had with Doug. "Can I chant about a relationship?"

"Absolutely," Hanako said. "You can chant about anything."

Scott said, "It's time to end. We'll continue this discussion same time same place, next week. Let's do sancho, chant Nam-myoho-renge-kyo three times." They all faced the Gohonzon.

When they were finished Hanako came up to Nancy. "Would you like to exchange phone numbers? Then if you have questions or want to chant with someone, we could be in touch."

"I'd like that," Nancy said. Lisa told Hanako both of them would be there the following week.

As Nancy looked around the room, she could see that people were there from all walks of life and with varying degrees of experience. They seemed peaceful and happy and from what she had seen of the group, they were all chanting about everything in their lives. She felt a sudden rush of excitement as she realized she wanted to try the experiment. What if chanting actually worked?

To the Reader

Setting Goals

We left Nancy getting ready to set her first goal. Maybe you are thinking of trying to chant for something yourself. If so, consider taking the ninety-day challenge. That means you pick a goal that is a stretch for you and chant for it for ninety days.

You can chant for anything you like. At the beginning, people often chant for concrete goals, because then it's easy to know when you have have achieved one. Also, when you begin to chant, certain problems feel like a priority, so start with them.

You can chant for as many goals as you like. Some people have lists of goals.

Let's look at the kinds of things Nancy might chant about regarding her relationship problem. She could chant for a harmonious relationship. She might chant for Doug's happiness. She could chant for a solution to their fighting. She could chant for clarity about the relationship or for a solution regarding his drinking. She could chant to know whether she should stay in the relationship.

Other goals might include chanting to be enlightened, or to have a peaceful heart, or for world peace. You could chant for a certain amount of money to meet an obligation by a certain date. You could chant for anything, depending upon what is needed in your life. Even if you don't chant for a specific goal, your life will be pulled in a positive direction. It just might take longer to happen.

When you formulate a goal, make sure you state it as what you want. For example let's say you want to lose twenty pounds. Don't chant to lose the weight. That's a negative goal. Chant to weigh your goal weight. If you're trying to cope with anxiety, don't chant to get rid of the anxiety, chant for inner peace.

When you decide to chant about something, it is important to recognize there is a big difference between *hoping* it will happen and making a determination that it *will* happen and that you will do whatever is necessary to see that it does. You may not see much happen if you just hope for something but don't really believe it will happen.

In Western culture, we are taught to strategize about how a goal will be accomplished. When you use this practice and chant for a goal, understand that all you have to do is set the goal and stay focused on the solution. Let the universe handle everything else. At first it may seem strange to set the goal and not to try to figure it out. Remember Suzanne's experience.

Guidelines for Setting Goals

- Always set a positive goal. State it as: "I want to weigh 140 pounds," *not*, "want to lose twenty five pounds."
- See the goal as completed.
- Don't strategize about how you are going to get there. That's the responsibility of the universe. You stay focused on the completed goal, what you want.
- Make a determination you will absolutely achieve your goal. There is a big difference between a hope and a determination.
- Once you set the goal, pay attention to ideas that come to you, as they represent the universe responding to your intention.

- Take action on the ideas you receive, which relate to your goal.
- Chant until you achieve your goal.
- And—Enjoy the adventure.

8

Change Brings Resistance

Nancy slipped back into the apartment at about 9:00 p.m. She was exhilarated by the meeting but also nervous about Doug. How was he going to respond to her having gone out?

When she opened the door he was waiting for her, wine glass in hand. His eyes were bloodshot and the smell of wine was thick on the air. Her heart sank. She hated the smell of alcohol. It always meant he would be unreasonable. She didn't need that tonight.

Doug looked upset. "So you're finally home."

"I wasn't gone long," Nancy said defensively. "I just needed to do something I'm interested in."

"Who was that woman with you?"

"You mean Lisa? She's a friend of mine at work."

"Where did you go?"

"To the Buddhist center." She smiled. "I can't wait to tell you all about it."

Doug interrupted with a skeptical look. "Why didn't you tell me where you were going?"

Nancy looked directly at Doug. "I did tell you. I said I was going to a meeting." *Do I have to get your permission for everything?* Her anticipation at sharing what had happened in the meeting and her enjoyment both vanished.

"I didn't think you'd be interested," she said out loud. *I thought you might try to persuade me not to go.*

"Who'd you meet over there?" He shot her a sharp glance.

Nancy sighed. There was Doug, being jealous again. She knew he wanted to find out if she had met some man over at the center.

"No one in particular. Don't you want to hear what happened?"

"No I don't really want to hear," he said, dismissively. "Frankly I think it sounds kooky, like those people in robes and things. I don't like you going off half-cocked."

Although Nancy felt guilty for upsetting Doug, she also felt irritated. It was always like this, any time she wanted to do something on her own. Doug always put her down for it. It was getting to the point that she wasn't sure she trusted her own judgment anymore. And, if he wasn't putting her down for something else, that jealousy was there. At the beginning she had been flattered by it, thought it meant she was special. Now it was a problem. He couldn't leave it alone.

She tried to placate him. "Come on Doug. Don't be like that. It was just people like you and me."

"You've let me worry all evening and now you tell me to leave it alone?" His voice rose. "You don't need anything like this. Religion's just a crutch."

Nancy protested. "It's not a crutch. Those people didn't seem like the kind of people who need crutches. I thought they were strong. Look at this." She gave him the pamphlet and some of the introductory materials the group had given her.

He pushed her hand aside. "I'm really not interested in hearing about it."

"But you don't know anything about it."

He ignored her comment. "I'm afraid you're not being discriminating."

That was in the past. Wasn't it? She'd been taken in when that salesman tried to sell her the stove. Maybe she *was* being taken in this time too. She started to doubt herself. "Now Doug . . . "

"You left after I expressly asked you not to. I get so upset with you!" Without warning, he whirled and punched the wall. His fist went right through the wall board.

"What do you think you're doing?" Nancy cried.

Doug looked shocked. He pulled his fist out of the hole.

"I guess I just lost it." He put an arm around her. "When you do things after I ask you not to, it just drives me crazy." The smell of wine enveloped her.

"But I have interests too and they might not be the same as yours."

"Don't start, Nancy," Doug warned.

She hesitated, looked at his determined face, and decided she had gone as far as she could this time. She couldn't talk with him when he'd been drinking. She turned, went into the bedroom and closed the door.

Nancy lay awake a long time. She pretended to be asleep when Doug came to bed and remained unresponsive when he put an arm around her.

If he was so upset about the practice, she wasn't sure she could continue to pursue it. Was it worth it to upset him so much, or should she do it in spite of his feelings to show him he couldn't control her this way? She was afraid if she made him too angry, he might decide to leave her. She tossed and turned, the question unresolved. She'd talk with Lisa tomorrow. Finally, she fell into a restless sleep.

At 7:30 a.m. her eyes flew open. A shot of adrenalin flooded her body. She had to be at work at 8:00. She couldn't be late or Annette would have her hide. She took a quick shower.

At 7:58 she slipped into her office chair with a sense of relief. She'd made it, even having put on make-up. Lisa gave her a smile.

"Want to take a walk at break?"

"Love it," said Nancy. They bent to their computers.

At 10:30 a.m. both the young women stepped onto the bike path, which ran along the east side of the agency. "How was it when you got home last night?" Lisa asked.

Nancy let out a breath. "Doug was mad. When he found out I'd gone to the Buddhist center, he tried to argue me out of it. He thinks I'm being taken in."

Lisa kept up the pace. "How do *you* feel?"

Nancy took several more steps before answering. She didn't want to hurt Lisa's feelings, but she may as well know the truth. "I don't know whether I can continue with the practice, since he's so against it."

"I think we'd better talk with Hanako about this," said Lisa. "I'm so new I don't really know what Buddhists would advise you to do in a situation like this."

"I can talk with her, but I'm not sure what I'm going to do. This isn't anything I expected."

"I know. We'll go together."

Nancy felt reassured. Even though she didn't know Lisa well, she liked her a lot. She was glad she didn't have to talk to Hanako by herself.

When they returned to the agency, Lisa and Nancy went to look for Annette. "If we ate lunch at our desks while continuing to work, could we leave a half an hour early?" asked Lisa.

Annette hesitated, then frowned, "Don't make a habit of it, but I guess once would be okay."

Lisa went to call Hanako. Nancy felt relieved. If they left at four and Doug didn't get home until his usual time at six, they'd have time to discuss the situation. When Lisa returned she nodded. "She'll be expecting us." The two women returned to work.

To the Reader

Using the Chant to Overcome Resistance

Nancy has made a tentative decision to change her life and Doug is putting up major resistance. You've probably experienced resistance whenever you've begun to change in some way, whether by taking on a new project or trying to develop a new more positive habit, or to change a relationship.

If you are trying to change a relationship, the other person or people in the family are going to want you to go back to the way you were before. Everyone is familiar with the status quo, knowing what to expect. Change brings anxiety. This is particularly true when only one person wants to make the change and the other person likes things the way they are.

The clear inspiration of a new start can bog down with the reality of doing something differently. Many people give up at this point, rather than persisting through blocks and giving themselves a chance to grow through the process.

The beginning of change brings resistance in the form of personal fears and anxieties. For many, it's easier to just let things stay as they are rather than experience these uncomfortable feelings.

You learned in the new people's meeting that you have both a light and a dark side. The negative side obscures the fact that you can have your life as you want it when you connect with your Buddha nature. That negativity invariably will be triggered when you stand at the beginning of change.

It's important to remember that resistance to change is normal. If you persist in moving forward, eventually the resistance will disappear before the new reality.

You will find that overcoming obstacles brings growth in your own life when you are basing the change on chanting Nam-myoho-renge-kyo. As you overcome one obstacle after another, you move step-by-step toward living as you were meant to live, using your full potential.

9

Poison Into Medicine

That day, at 4:15 p.m., Nancy and Lisa knocked on Hanako's door. She smiled and immediately took Nancy into a hug and then hugged Lisa too. A lump came into Nancy's throat. Hanako's kindness relaxed some wall within her.

When Nancy walked into the living room she saw what she guessed was a carved butsudan with a black satin finish. It looked Asian. Pillows on the couch were quilted in Asian fabrics as well.

"How beautiful," she exclaimed. For a moment she forgot why she had come, and picked up one to examine it. "Did you make these?"

Hanako's eyes took on a sparkle. "I've taken a quilting class and love doing it. You should try it some time."

"Maybe I will." She gestured toward the front of the room. Is that a butsudan?" Hanako nodded and opened the doors to show her a Gohonzon, which had a blue-green background rather than the gold of the large one at the community center. It was quite a bit smaller.

"This is what an individual's Gohonzon looks like. You can get one for your own home, when you are chanting regularly."

"I'm thinking about getting one," said Lisa.

Nancy couldn't imagine what Doug would do if she got one of those.

Hanako brought out green tea in small cups with a bamboo design. She set the lacquered tray on the coffee table. Lisa took a chair and Nancy settled on the couch.

"Now, tell me what happened," said Hanako.

With a rush of words and tears, Nancy described the fight that had happened last night after she went home. She concluded, "I don't think I can continue with the practice."

"Did Lisa tell you that there have been other women who have started out with problems like yours?"

"No." Nancy shook her head. "We haven't had time to discuss it. Were their problems as bad as mine?"

Hanako's voice was calm and warm. "Oh yes. I can tell you several experiences I've heard. Today the lives of those women are completely different. We call it turning poison into medicine."

"I like that idea," Nancy said. "How do you go about doing it?"

"Your problem with Doug is a good place to begin. We're going to sit down and chant together for a solution to your problem."

Nancy felt dubious. She couldn't see how chanting would change Doug's behavior. But, after all, this was an experiment. She'd try it and see what happened.

All three women faced the Gohonzon. Hanako turned to Nancy. "We need to set a goal here, so we'll all know what to chant for. What do you want to see happen?"

Nancy thought carefully for a few moments. "I want Doug to stop drinking. He's drinking too much and when he drinks, he has a temper. Last night, he hit the wall and put his hand right through it. I was afraid he was going to hit me. The problem is, I'm pregnant and I don't think I can leave him."

"Does Doug know that you're pregnant?" Hanako asked.

Nancy shook her head. "I just found out myself and haven't told him yet. After what happened last night, I'm not sure I want him to know." She put her face in her hands.

Hanako thought for a moment. "Chanting for Doug to stop drinking is a clear goal. But you have other concerns too. How about chanting for clarity about what to do, for your protection, and also for a resolution to the problem?"

"That sounds right to me," Nancy said.

"One other thing," Hanako said. "You should chant for Doug's happiness."

Lisa nodded. "That sounds like a good idea. I don't think people act this way when they are happy." That made sense to Nancy.

"What you're doing as we chant is to activate the wisdom you have available inside of you," Hanako added. "It's a much deeper wisdom and you can get answers to your problem from a much more profound level." Nancy hoped she was right.

All three women faced the Gohonzon. Hanako laced her beads through her fingers, tapped the bell and slowly chanted Nam-myoho-renge-kyo three times, motioning to Nancy and Lisa to join her. They both followed her lead, repeatedly chanting Nam-myoho-renge-kyo.

As Nancy chanted for clarity, her mind moved from one aspect of the problem to another. She belatedly recognized that Doug was worried about his job. He had said something which she had dismissed. Maybe that's why he'd been so short-tempered lately.

She noted the increase in Doug's drinking and recognized that this was making everything else worse. She focused on chanting for his happiness. Maybe if he were happy he wouldn't drink so much. Then she moved to chanting for her protection and for a resolution to their problem. She felt herself relax and was startled when Hanako rang the bell to bring the session to an end. She was surprised to find they had chanted for half an hour.

"When you go home, chant about this for a few minutes a couple times a day. Try to be consistent about doing it," Hanako said. "Since you're just beginning, I know I'm asking a lot of you, but you need to overcome this karma."

"What is karma?" Nancy asked.

"We'll get into it as time goes on, but for now just chant with the goal in mind and don't give up until you get it. Both Lisa and I will chant for you too. Call us whenever you need to and we can talk or chant together."

On the way home, Nancy thought of how the two women had handled her problem. They didn't try to give her solutions and hadn't judged her. They didn't seem to judge Doug either, but seemed to have some understanding which Nancy didn't have yet. She wanted to find out what it was. She had hope that maybe—just maybe—she'd be able to resolve this situation even though she couldn't see how. She'd try this chanting, since she didn't know what else to do, and the members seemed so sure it would make a difference. She wasn't going to chant while Doug was around. She didn't want to trigger another fight.

To the Reader

Turning Around Adverse Circumstances

Nancy happens to have a relationship problem. Using Nancy's example, Hanako has shown how to handle any kind of problem using the practice. Maybe you are dealing with financial issues, or a problem with your employer, or a quandary with a child. Whatever the concern might be, the first step toward handling it starts with clarifying the best resolution from your point of view. Make sure your desired resolution is clear and that you aren't holding back.

What does holding back mean? One member had Multiple Sclerosis. To date, MS has been thought to be incurable. She chanted in a vague way because she didn't want to seriously get her hopes up that the MS might be resolved, and then be disappointed. In other words, she didn't believe she had the power within herself to overcome the problem. As long as she chanted this way, nothing much happened.

Her sponsor saw she wasn't moving forward and advised her to chant that the MS would stop its progression. He also advised her to make a determination to do whatever was necessary to achieve that goal. When she chanted in that manner, she got the results she wanted. She went through a highly controversial treatment which stopped the progression of the MS.

Sometimes less-than-sure or half-hearted beliefs about what's possible can stop you from really admitting what you want. Until you clarify your true wishes, there will be halfway results.

The first step to turning poison into medicine is to understand that you are a Buddha. This means you can function from the highest level of life existing within a human being. You have a beautiful center core which connects with everything in the universe. When you tap into this level of life, a deeper wisdom becomes accessible to you, helping you to understand and handle life problems. Chanting Nam-myoho-renge-kyo will access this level for you.

You will find that invisible connections are made to fulfill your goal. For that reason, since you cannot possibly know how you will reach your goal, you must maintain an open mind. In this culture we are taught to strategize about a problem. Instead, chant about it first.

One forty-three-year practitioner has a track record of always achieving the goals she sets, even though they might appear impossible on the surface of life. She doesn't entertain any thoughts about why she can't have what she wants. Instead she just chants for what she wants. Against all outward appearances, which would indicate her goal is impossible, she achieves her goal.

In order for this to be successful, you have to be of one mind about what you want, not unsure about whether your goal is the right thing. It is worthwhile to take extra time to truly clarify what you want, so you can be clearly one-pointed when you chant about it.

A Buddha is not some higher being different from us, although that is a popular conception. A Buddha functions at the highest level of human potential, doing the Buddha's work to relieve suffering, while living in everyday life. Anyone can do this.

You do not have to go to a mountaintop or become a monk and retreat from life. You can do it exactly as you are, by chanting on a daily basis. You don't become a Buddha many lifetimes from now and stay there forever. Rather, you tap that level of life in yourself on a daily basis.

When you function in the lesser self by strategizing, you are using your mind rather than accessing your Buddha nature. It is like trying to take the water of wisdom out of a lake with a small soup ladle. This is why it seems so hard to overcome some problems.

When you chant, *you become the lake* and have access to whatever you need to handle problems in life. Then problems seem to resolve themselves as you take whatever actions seem necessary to move in the direction of your goal.

Steps to "Turn Poison Into Medicine"

1. Know that your Buddha nature, your higher self, can find the solution to any problem.

2. Have faith, even if you don't know how it will happen, you will find the solution to your goal.

3. Tap your internal wisdom by chanting Nam-myoho-renge-kyo with a clear positive goal in mind. See it as completed.

4. Chant with the determination that this problem, without question, will be resolved. You are not a supplicant.

5. Do not entertain thoughts which would indicate your goal cannot be achieved. Just chant for what you truly want.

6. Keep chanting until the problem is resolved.

10

The Start of the Experiment

Nancy climbed out of Lisa's car in front of her apartment. She felt curiously comforted, as though she was not alone in facing this problem. She felt stronger and more peaceful. She remembered that Doug had a meeting at work, so he wouldn't be home early. She decided to take advantage of the time to herself to start her ninety-day challenge.

She resolved to do what Hanako had told her to do, chant for a couple of periods during the day. She had set several goals: one, to develop clarity about what was happening in the relationship; two, to resolve the problems in their relationship; and three, to become stronger herself.

She looked around their apartment. Where could she sit? One wall had the big bay window looking out on the park and the dining room cabinet and china cabinet were on the other end. She guessed she could sit on the couch. But she didn't have a Gohonzon. She fished Hanako's phone number out of her pocket.

"Hanako, it's Nancy. I want to try chanting for my goals but I don't have a Gohonzon. I don't know how I'm supposed to arrange the room."

"I'm glad you're decided to challenge the problem," said Hanako. Nancy could hear the warmth in her voice. "Do you have a comfortable chair that you could face toward a blank place on a wall?"

Nancy looked around the blue and gold room. "I think the couch could work."

"Great. Just visualize a focal point in the blank space. That represents the Gohonzon, your Buddha nature, inside you. Then think of your goal and chant Nam-myo-ho-renge-kyo for as long as you wish. Usually I chant until I feel there's been a resolution."

"Even though I just finished chanting with you, I still have a question. Do I have to keep my mind on the goal the whole time?"

"No. Start with your intention in mind and then let whatever happens, happen. It's fine if other thoughts come. I get some of my best answers to problems when thoughts come spontaneously like that. This isn't like other kinds of meditation where people try to clear their minds."

"Thanks Hanako." Nancy hung up and settled herself comfortably on the couch. She didn't know what to expect.

She turned her attention to her goal and picked up the chant. At first she had to remember the pronunciation of Nam-myoho-renge-kyo, and found initially it was hard to focus on the goal. Then gradually the words came more easily and she didn't have to focus so much on the pronunciation. She relaxed into the rhythm.

Her mind turned to last night's fight with Doug. It'd started when she'd said she wanted to go out and do something for herself. The few other times she'd said she'd wanted to do something, he hadn't taken it well. But when she'd done what he wanted, no problems.

With a start she realized she'd almost stopped speaking her mind, especially if she thought Doug would disagree. She shifted uneasily.

Her gaze turned to the window. What if she could never be herself with Doug? Her mother had let her father be dominant. She'd always thought that was just the way things were. She became aware her gaze had moved and pulled her attention back to her focal point on the wall.

Do I want a relationship like Mom and Dad's, or do I want a relationship more like partners? She stretched her legs and curled them back under her. She pondered this question for a moment.

Then, to her surprise, she realized she wanted to be more like partners. She hadn't seen that coming. Sadness crept over her. *It's going to be pretty hard to be partners if Doug loses his temper whenever I want to do something that's important to me.*

Her throat felt dry. She stopped the chant and walked to the kitchen to get a glass of water. She re-settled herself and picked up the chant again.

What would she do when Doug came home? Pretend like nothing happened, or say something? In the past she'd pretty much just let things go, or had tried hard to get back on his good side by giving up what she wanted to do.

Not this time, she thought. Immediately she felt nervous. What if he hit her instead of the wall? He'd come close last night. But, she reminded herself, he hadn't hit her. Yet.

She decided to add another goal. She'd chant for protection. Would Lisa let her come to her house if Doug got drunk and threatened her? She'd call her after she finished chanting. Five more minutes. When she ended she felt peaceful and connected. She was feeling more confident as well.

She phoned Lisa.

Nancy said, "Thanks so much for taking me to see Hanako."

"I'm delighted you would go with me."

Nancy bit her lip, but then remembered her new-found confidence. "I have a question for you. You can say no if you want."

"What is it?" asked Lisa.

"I just finished chanting. If Doug went off the wall, could I come to your place? Just until I figured out what to do?"

After a brief pause, Lisa said warmly, "Of course."

Nancy sighed with relief. "Thanks. I hope I never need to come over, but I really appreciate your being willing. I'll see you tomorrow."

Being able to go to Lisa's gave Nancy an escape should anything else happen. She had to prepare herself, since she had someone else to protect as well as herself. A warm feeling came over her as she thought about the baby.

What about Doug? When should she tell him? She mulled the question and then came to a reluctant decision. For now she wouldn't tell him about the pregnancy. She'd wait and see what happened with the relationship first.

At eight p.m., the door abruptly opened and Doug walked in. He was carrying a dozen roses over his arm. Nancy involuntarily winced. "I didn't expect you home until nine!"

A look of shame crossed his face. "I'm sorry," he said quietly.

"So am I," Nancy said.

He held out the roses to her. She just let him stand there and didn't try to take them.

"Please," he pleaded, thrusting the bouquet at her. Those imploring eyes again. She was tempted. She started to reach for the flowers, but pulled her hand back.

"If I do, you're going to think I've forgiven you," she said, crossing her arms.

Doug's shoulders slumped. "I don't know why I do these things. It's like something gets into me. I was drunk." He looked away.

Nancy reached inside herself, drawing out courage she didn't know she had. "Yes, and this doesn't happen when you are sober. You've never been violent before. I thought you were going to hit me!" She burst into tears. "I was scared."

His mouth opened in surprise and his eyes widened. "I'd never, you don't really think I'd hit you!" He stared at her intently. "Do you?"

She paused but then plowed ahead. "I don't know what to think. You scared me." Nancy wiped her eyes.

Doug reached out to take her in his arms, but Nancy stepped back. He let his arms drop to his sides. "I'm afraid I'm going to lose my job," he said. "We're having layoffs at the office. I guess my temper is worse because of the tension." Doug hung his head. "What can I do to make it up to you?"

Nancy was amazed. Doug had never acted contrite like this before. She had a brief rush of exhilaration. Maybe they *could* work it out. She remembered Hanako saying that she might have to take action and do something different. Fear flashed through her but she remained calm. She said quietly, "I want to learn more about this Buddhism."

He scowled.

He didn't want to change at all. She said, "I don't think you really want to change anything. You just want me to forgive you and then we go back to the way things were before."

He looked as though he had chewed on a lemon. "I'll try. That's the best I can do. Will you take these now?"

She reluctantly extended her hand for the roses.

To the Reader

Chanting at Home

As you have seen, Hanako advised Nancy to find a comfortable place to sit. She directed her to imagine a focal point on a blank space on the wall. This represented the Gohonzon inside of her. Then she advised her to chant Nam-myoho-renge-kyo for as long as she wished. If this is your first chanting session, you might try what Nancy did.

You don't have to keep your mind on the goal for the whole time. Just visualize your intention, your completed goal at the beginning of the session, and then let your mind go wherever it wishes. Deeper insights might come to you. Ideas for actions you might take toward your goal could pop into your mind. Let them come and don't critique them. You can evaluate what has come up later when you have finished your chanting session.

Sometimes you might receive very specific ideas on ways to solve your situation. While one practitioner was doing the work of remodeling his fixer-upper home, he used to chant for solutions to construction problems. Inevitably, the ideas which came to him worked better than anything he'd thought up by himself.

Sometimes we don't get any ideas regarding the goal while actually chanting, but in the next day or two, information comes from some other source. A book might show up, or a person might have just the information you need.

Don't try to force anything to happen. Just stay comfortable and easy, allowing whatever happens to happen. Renew your intention at the beginning of the next chanting session.

When you chant about a goal, you are having a conversation with the universe. You set the goal and then the universe responds. Pay attention to anything which shows up pertaining to the goal you are chanting about.

Frequently while sitting before the Gohonzon, ideas and insights might come to you about how you might change the way you are handling your situation. You might want to try some of those ideas. Remember if nothing changes, nothing changes. We can't hold on to our old ways of doing things and expect something to change.

Sometimes the solutions to problems take several weeks to appear. Never give up chanting for your goal. Something will happen sooner or later. Count on it. Just keep envisioning the completed goal and don't let your mind slip into negativity.

Even though you might not have achieved your specific goal yet, your life has started to move forward in a positive direction. You, like Bill in the introductory meeting, are laying a foundation. Pay attention to the steps of progress. When a goal is set, usually one of these things happen.

1. You will get the goal.

2. You won't get the specific goal you were chanting for but something will happen which meets your needs even better.

3. You won't get the goal but will understand why. An example of this was a young couple who put their house on the market thinking they would sell it to take a job out of town. They had remod-

eled and decorated the house and it was perfect for them. The house didn't sell, although other houses on their street were selling. When the husband landed a job out of town, they didn't have to move. The new position's only requirement, which they met, was that they live within fifteen minutes of an airport.

4. You will get the goal you thought you wanted but there will be some kind of unexpected lesson connected with it. One young woman started the practice at age eighteen, during her hippie days. She chanted for pot. She got the pot but then realized that, compared to chanting, it brought her down. A couple of experiences like this and she gave up the pot.

If the latter occurs, remind yourself that you have gotten exactly what you need for your growth and ask yourself what you need to learn in this situation. Frequently these experiences lead to deeper self-knowledge.

You may find you have doubts. Doubt is entirely normal. Usually, no one at the beginning believes they really have a Buddha nature. That conviction doesn't come until you have used the practice and overcome many obstacles you originally thought were impossible.

If you need chanting support, or someone with whom to discuss your doubts, you can always call your sponsor or someone you have met in one of the meetings. The group is there to support people who are challenging the problems in their lives. After all, we all need support at one time or another.

- This is an experiential practice.
- If you haven't started, try the ninety-day challenge.
- Prove it to yourself.

BONUS DOWNLOAD
For readers of this book

The Key Steps to Chanting

Get your copy here:

www.margaretblaine.com/keysteps

⚜11⚜

The Ten Worlds: The Four Higher Worlds

Saturday morning, Hanako called at nine. Fortunately Doug had gone out to get a paper, so Nancy didn't have to explain who it was.

Hanako asked, "How did it go yesterday?"

A swell of energy washed over Nancy. "I couldn't believe it. I'd just finished chanting when Doug came home. He had brought me some roses and was very repentant." She bit her lip. "I don't know though. Other times he's been sorry after he's lost it. And lately, when he's been drinking, it's like he's a different person."

"One step at a time," Hanako said. "Now that you're working on changing your situation, I want to take you to a district meeting next week. We'll discuss the ten worlds."

"Is it a day or evening meeting?" asked Nancy.

"Does it matter?"

Nancy paused. "It's much harder to go out by myself in the evening."

"Why don't you invite Doug?" Hanako suggested. "He'll get to know us and see he doesn't have to worry."

Nancy laughed involuntarily. "You don't know Doug. I'll ask him, but I don't think he'll come."

That evening Nancy invited him to go to the meeting with her the following week.

He shook his head. "Maybe you want to learn about this, but count me out. I don't want to go."

A week later, Hanako drove Nancy to the district meeting. To Nancy's surprise, Doug hadn't fought with her about her spending the evening without him. *Maybe he is trying after all.*

Hanako seemed relaxed behind the wheel. Nancy enjoyed the soft late light of the early spring evening. The trees were just budding out and the air smelled of spring and flowers.

Nancy inhaled the fragrant lilac scent. "What kind of meeting is this? I can't remember what you said."

Hanako glanced at Nancy. "This is a district meeting. It's like a home group within the SGI, our larger international organization. It's different from the new people's group in that almost everyone has decided that the practice is for them, and they are chanting on a daily basis."

"I hope I know enough to understand what's going on."

"Don't worry. One of the members will have prepared something on the topic and then everyone joins in with their thoughts and ideas. You can join in or simply observe. It's up to you."

Nancy relaxed. At least she wouldn't be put on the spot. "It sounds more informal than other groups I've seen. In those, the leader is much more like a guru."

Hanako chuckled. "You're right, it's totally different. In the SGI there are only people with more and less experience. No one is a guru. Everyone is encouraged to teach to the best of their ability." She turned into the parking lot. "It's great, because the experienced members help teach the newer ones both individually and in discussion groups. Everyone's welcome to participate. The whole point is to encourage each person in his or her practice."

"Kind of like the new people's group," said Nancy, climbing out of the passenger seat.

Hanako nodded and locked the car. "We'll start with *gongyo* at the beginning just like before. Did you bring your *gongyo* book?"

Nancy frowned, ashamed. "I'm afraid I forgot it."

"That's okay. I have one. We'll share."

When they opened the door to the meeting, a smiling woman hurried to bring chairs for them. People sat chanting in front of a smaller Gohonzon, like Hanako's. About fifteen to twenty people filled the room. The two of them settled down in the back row of chairs. Nancy liked the fact that no one paid attention to her and she had time to look around the room.

The living room was blue and green. Calming colors. The windows looked out over a lawn bordered by woods. The owners must be peaceful inside to have such a harmonious environment, she thought.

Nancy came back to the present as she recognized the chant. *So they always started with Nam-myoho-renge-kyo. She could do that.* She put her palms together, focused on the Gohonzon and started to chant Nam-myoho-renge-kyo.

The man leading the chant tapped a bell in front of the Gohonzon three times. There was a pause. Nancy looked at Hanako to see what was expected. Hanako brought out the *gongyo* book and pointed to the line where they would begin the recitation of the Lotus Sutra. Nancy listened and tried to keep up, but the Chinese words were hard to follow. This would take a while to learn, she thought. She fumbled with the words and rhythm but followed Hanako's finger as best she could. When they finished, Hanako whispered, "You did great."

The group pulled together a circle of chairs. People quickly introduced themselves by first names. The members looked as though they came from all kinds of different backgrounds: a couple of Japanese women, and a young man who looked Hispanic. One woman even carried a baby. Everyone seemed comfortable with diversity. Nancy liked that.

A balding middle-aged man introduced himself as Curt, and brought out some notes. He looked around at everyone. "Tonight we're going to continue the discussion on the ten worlds. Last time we covered the lower six worlds. This time we'll discuss the four higher worlds. After a brief presentation we'll have a group discussion." There was a rustle as everyone settled in to listen. Nancy noted his blue shirt and grey slacks. He looked conservative.

Curt glanced around the room. "The important thing to remember about the ten worlds is that these worlds are inner potentials, not places outside of us. We move in and out of them all day long as we respond to circumstances in our lives."

Curt turned a diagram around to show the ten worlds. He used a pointer to indicate each one. "Tonight I'll quickly go over the lower six worlds to begin:

Hell – (stuck, miserable)

Hunger – (unfulfilled cravings)

Animality – (law of the jungle)

Anger – (arrogance, jealousy)

Humanity – (neutral, calm)

Rapture – (temporary, outer happiness)

The lower six worlds are also called the six evil paths and they can readily lead to suffering."

A young woman wearing jeans commented. "I've been noticing the lower worlds in my life this last week. I do move in and out of them."

Curt nodded. "We'll all find that happening, if we pay attention." He held up another poster that read *Mutual Possession of the Ten Worlds*. "This means that each of the ten worlds has all the potentials of the other nine within it. That means we can, at will, pull ourselves out of a lower world and into a higher one."

"What are the higher ones?" asked Nancy. "These all look pretty negative except for the top two."

"I'm Carlos," said a young Hispanic man. Curt gave him the floor. "I'll try to explain." He leaned forward and ticked them off on his fingers. "They are:

Learning – (learning from others)

Realization – (discovery from personal experience, creativity)

Bodhisattva – (compassion, working to help others become happy)

Buddhahood – (unshakeable happiness, freedom, realization of the true nature of life, working to relieve the suffering of people)"

Nancy thought those sounded like much more positive worlds.

Carlos continued. "To enter the higher worlds you have to take action." He paused. "You don't just react to something as you do in the lower worlds."

Hanako jumped into the discussion. "Let's say you're feeling stuck and depressed. You can sit to chant and pull yourself into one of the higher worlds or at least to a more positive side of a lower world."

A red haired girl interjected, "What do you mean by the positive side of a lower world?"

Hanako gestured for emphasis. "Let's say you are furious about an injustice in the world, and are living in the world of anger. If you chant about it, that anger will transmute to a desire to get justice done and you'll see you might take action. That pulls you out of the negative and into something more constructive."

Aha, Nancy thought. That makes sense.

Another woman added, "The great thing about the ten worlds is that even though you are going through something difficult, you can pull yourself out of being stuck in the negativity of that world. So you can always live a happier life."

"That's been very important to me," Carlos said. "When I started the practice, I suffered from depression and then I got a job where I was totally burned out. In order to cope, I chanted until I felt a smile come over my face. When that smile came I knew I could face the day, no matter what."

Nancy turned to him. "Are you still in the job?"

Carlos shook his head. "No, I chanted hard for a job that would suit me better, and now I'm much happier in the new one."

Nancy immediately thought of her own job. Was it actually possible to chant for a new position at work?

As they were driving home after the meeting, Hanako asked, "What did you think of the discussion?"

"It was really interesting," Nancy said with enthusiasm. "I see what you mean when you say you can learn a lot at the district meetings." Hanako glanced at her with a knowing smile.

"I want to continue coming to meetings." Nancy could hardly believe what she'd just said.

What would Doug's reaction be? He wouldn't be happy about it, that much was obvious. He might be trying to improve his attitude, but he still got angry whenever she made a decision on her own. She felt a little anxious, but then squared her shoulders.

She turned to Hanako. "I feel better when I chant. I'm going to see how the ninety-day experiment works out."

"Good for you," said Hanako.

To the Reader

Using the Chant to Change
Your Life Condition

The discussion about the ten worlds shows you the possibility of using the chant proactively in order to shift your life condition from one of the lower worlds into a higher level of that world, or into one of the higher worlds. You've seen that Nancy felt more confident after she chanted. Being able to pull yourself out of negativity is one of the benefits of practicing.

Here's an example. A woman in the practice moved into a position in the SGI where she assumed responsibility for supporting a number of people in the group. All her life, she'd been something of a loner. She'd never used the phone to connect with people, but waited for people to call her. Initially, after taking the position, she didn't call anyone out of fear of being rejected. Then, one day she realized that this was part of her responsibility, and she must deal with her fear of calling.

For a while after she took the position, although she chanted consistently, her fear didn't change. One day she discovered, to her surprise, that when she'd chanted for an hour, she felt much more self-confident when the session ended. She made it her practice to go and do her calls right away.

After handling her reluctance in this way for a while, she realized that by reaching out, she was making friends and bringing some wonderful people into her life. At that point she lost her fear altogether. For the first time, she felt connected with other women. This was one of the great benefits of her practice.

Other people have used the practice to handle anxiety in the middle of the night when they can't sleep. They lie in bed and chant for a while, until their anxiety lessens and they are able to fall asleep. A five-year practitioner told the group that he'd suffered from anxiety all of his life. After chanting for a couple of years, the anxiety left him altogether. Today he radiates well-being.

If you suffer from something like a long-standing depression, it may take longer to overcome. But many SGI members who started practicing with a history of depression have overcome it and are happy today. As you saw, Carlos pulled himself out of depression so he could go to work. This can happen for you too.

Over time, with consistent daily practice, your life condition will spontaneously remain in the higher worlds more and more of the time.

In one discussion, during a district meeting, members talked about how happiness had come to stay in their lives. At first, it seemed they became happier and then it ebbed rather like the tide. Then, when the next wave of happiness came, it stayed longer and was deeper. Finally the full tide came in and they have remained happy, regardless of what is happening in the outer aspects of their lives.

This kind of happiness is different from the happiness of the world of Rapture. Rapture is based on temporary satisfaction and will depart when the satisfaction which stimulated it has run its course. Unlike Rapture, "full-tide" happiness is steady and will underlie anything happening on the surface of your life. It's unshakeable happiness.

A new member recently observed that when she began practicing she recognized she hadn't been happy for fifteen years. Even though she still struggles with some financial problems, she reports she is happy for the first time in a long, long time.

If you are trying the ninety-day challenge to prove the practice to yourself, you might want to try working with the chant to change your life condition. For example, you might set a goal of being confident. Then you begin to chant for that goal. Remember to chant for confidence, since that is what you want to experience. Keep chanting for the goal, whether it takes a short or longer time to achieve. Once you feel confident, take the action you feared. You will feel a real glow at having overcome a characteristic which held you back.

This example may seem small, but these small steps, one after another, are the transformations which ultimately lead to enlightenment.

12

Obstacles Are Steps on the Path

When Nancy arrived home that evening, Doug was sitting in the recliner watching television. He was holding a gin and tonic and it didn't appear to be his first drink of the evening. He looked a little ragged around the edges. *He seems to be drinking more often.*

Doug didn't wait long to quiz her. "So what'd you think of it this time? Finally seen what it's all about?" He took a swallow of his drink and plunked it onto the side table.

Nancy hung up her coat and her purse. She wouldn't give him any ammunition. "It was a good meeting," she said simply. "People in that group are working hard on their lives."

He folded his arms in front of him. "What do you mean? You don't think we are?"

Nancy stiffened. "I didn't say that. I was just describing what the group was like." She didn't want to fight.

Doug said, "Yeah, right."

She put a hand on his arm. "Why don't you come with me and see what this group's all about? I'd love to have you come with me. There are some nice guys there. You might like them."

Doug looked uncomfortable. "You know I don't like to hang around with guys. I'd rather be with you."

"I was just thinking we could do something, you know, together." She gave him a hug.

Doug seemed to soften a bit. "Well, maybe." He drained the last of his drink.

The next day, Nancy set up a table with some candles below her focal point. If Doug didn't like it, she could take it down. She set a glass of water on the table, and lit the two candles.

She decided to chant while Doug was gone. It would be easier to avoid any conflict if he didn't actually see her chanting. She didn't know how he'd react when he saw what she'd done.

She set her intention as Hanako had told her to do. She reminded herself of her goals—increased clarity and protection, and for a resolution to the problem with Doug.

As she settled into the rhythm of the chant, her mind drifted to work and she realized she was skating on thin ice in the office. Lately, she hadn't been at her desk as much as she should have been. Instead, she'd been crying in the bathroom or going to doctor's appointments.

She straightened her back. *I want Annette to see me as responsible and capable, not as someone who can't handle her life.* She resolved to try to park her problems at the office door. She set a new goal, to be a competent, capable employee. If she had to support herself with the baby coming, being capable was going to be important. She took a sip of water.

Her mind went to Doug and their relationship. She had never felt comfortable with the way her parents handled their own decision making. She'd always wanted her mother to be more assertive. Nancy gasped. She'd let Doug dominate her in the same way her father had done with her mother.

She heard the door open and her newfound serenity fled. She heard Doug go into the kitchen and then the click of the refrigerator door opening.

Anxiety rose. *I guess he might as was well know that I'm continuing with the practice.* She heard Doug come into the room behind her.

"What are you doing?" he asked. "What's that table for?"

Nancy's breathing sped up. "Chanting." She gestured. "The table is my focal point."

He frowned. "I thought I told you how I feel about this chanting."

"You did." Nancy took a deep breath and reached deep inside for courage. "Maybe you don't remember, but I said that I wanted to explore it further."

Doug flushed. "So you're going to chant no matter how I feel about it?"

Nancy nodded. "I am." She felt guilty and also exhilarated. She began the chant again.

Doug paced behind her. She could feel his eyes on her. The hair on the back of her neck prickled. Finally, she couldn't stand it anymore. She swiveled her chair around. "What do you want?"

"You know what I want."

Nancy jumped up and faced him. "You can't have everything just because you want it." She froze, clapped her hand over her mouth. She couldn't believe she just said what she had thought for so long: it had just popped out. Shocked silence.

Doug's eyebrows raised and an expression of incredulity crossed his face. Her heart pounded. They stared at each other. Something in their relationship had changed.

Doug stepped back. "Where are you going?"

"I'm going to finish chanting in the bedroom. I'll close the door so I won't bother you." Nancy said. She couldn't let him get away with this. If she did, it would be like all the other times when she gave in and then put herself down for not standing up for what she wanted.

She snuffed the candles and stepped forward to pass him. He grabbed her arm. She stopped and just looked at him. "Don't try to stop me. I've given in to you over and over. This time I'm not going to."

He hesitated; then released her arm. Nancy walked to the bedroom and closed the door behind her. Her heart was pounding. It was hard to chant with Doug acting this way. She was glad she had held her own this time, but this was difficult.

The next morning she called Hanako. "Something happened yesterday and I'd like to talk with you about it."

"With Doug?"

"Yep. I'm not sure how to handle it."

"Let's meet at the market. It's a gorgeous day and I'd love to go." They agreed to meet at eleven.

When Nancy arrived at the outdoor Saturday market, the hustle and bustle of market activity soothed her, as did the clear, sunny, spring weather. Nothing like May in Oregon, she thought. Strolling along the sidewalk, she enjoyed looking at the colorful displays of vegetables. She spotted Hanako.

They walked slowly down the aisle, Hanako examining vegetables and putting them in her bag, as Nancy told her what had happened.

"Something like this is to be expected." Hanako seemed unperturbed. She picked up a head of lettuce.

"What do you mean by, 'to be expected'?"

Hanako smiled. "People who have practiced a few years all talk about it. When a person starts to chant to change their life, things happen to distract them from the practice. Have you ever heard the term sansho shima?"

"Yes, but I'm not sure what it means."

"You're seeing an example of it in Doug's behavior. When you start to chant, the darkness in your life and that of other people can be stirred up. It can result in hindrances to practice."

"That doesn't sound good," Nancy said.

Hanako's voice was soothing. "You don't need to worry about it. The chant will enable you to overcome any obstacle that might come up." Nancy slowly relaxed. She kept forgetting that. A feeling of reassurance crept over her.

Hanako looked directly at Nancy. "Remember, using the chant to overcome obstacles is the way you'll strengthen your life. We all have inner darkness and have to address it. It is what prevents us from becoming happy. The only way to become happy is to move through the obstacles. At least we have a way to live on the positive side of life."

Nancy tried not to think about Doug's reaction to her chanting the night before. She forced herself to look at Hanako. "How do you think I should chant about this? I can't imagine changing Doug's behavior by just chanting about it."

Hanako nodded. "I agree. It would be hard to chant to change someone else's behavior. I would chant for a resolution to the situation so you will be free to practice at home." Hanako reached for some onions.

A light bulb went on inside Nancy. "I see. So I should chant for what *I* want. I'm not necessarily chanting to change *his* behavior."

"Right," Hanako said.

Nancy felt hopeful. "Maybe something else might happen to make him feel better about the practice." She imagined Doug sitting next to her as they both chanted.

Hanako shrugged. "Maybe, maybe not. We never know how a solution to a problem will work out, so don't try to second-guess it. But the important thing is, don't ever let anyone or anything get between you and your Gohonzon. If you don't chant because you're uncomfortable, you've let him get in the way."

Nancy paused to examine a display of flowers. Hanako asked, "We talked about sansho shima, right?"

Nancy nodded.

"Let me give you some examples." Hanako held up her hand. She curled her fingers and raised her thumb. "Anytime you don't think you have time to chant, you are dealing with a hindrance. Think of things like distractions, worries, concerns, doubts, too much partying, friends who take you away from chanting or a meeting." She raised her second finger. "Other hindrances are over-commitment to work or school or being too busy. It's really easy to use these as excuses." She raised her third finger. "Another might be a person who resists your chanting or tries to make you doubt what you are doing."

Nancy gave a wry smile. "Sounds like I definitely have that one."

Hanako agreed. "I'd say so. Often the problem seems to fade away when you chant about it." She paused as if trying to think of others. Her fourth finger went up. "Ah yes. Sometimes you might come up against an obstacle which is so overwhelming you forget to chant or have so many doubts you can ever overcome it, you give up."

"I heard a story about a man who had so much pain from a kidney stone he forgot to chant. Like that?"

"Exactly," Hanako placed some bell peppers in her bag.

A fine coffee aroma reached Nancy's nose. Coffee would be wonderful. She looked around, and spotted the delectable odor's source. "Want to get a latte?" she asked.

Hanako paid for her vegetables. "I'd love to," she said. "My feet are tired."

As they turned into the coffeehouse, Nancy sniffed appreciatively. She loved the smell of perking coffee and fresh pastries. She examined the pastries under the glass counter. Biscotti would be perfect, she thought. They paid for their drinks and found a place to sit outside in order to enjoy the beautiful day. This is wonderful, thought Nancy, turning her face to the sun while savoring the taste of chocolate and orange.

After a few minutes of companionable silence, Hanako glanced at her watch, and looked startled. "It's later than I thought. I have an appointment at one. We'll talk tomorrow."

"Yes, thanks a lot, Hanako. You've been a big help and given me a lot to think about." Hanako smiled, her face softening with affection. Then she swept up her bags and headed toward her car.

Nancy remained in her chair, enjoying the hustle and bustle and sun. She certainly had been experiencing sansho shima. She'd stood up to Doug this last time, but she wondered how long it would be before she'd be able to chant without fighting with him. It was up to her not to let these distractions get between her and her practice.

To the Reader

Chanting to Overcome Obstacles

When you make the decision to start the practice, without being consciously aware of it, you have made the decision to break free of the sufferings of birth and death and gain enlightenment. As you have seen in the discussion on the ten worlds, each of us not only has an enlightened nature but also has the tendency to disbelieve it. This delusion is behind all human suffering, as most of us don't believe an individual can have his or her life as he or she wishes it to be.

Hanako has talked to Nancy about the fundamental darkness within each of us. Problems and obstacles arising out of this darkness can either act as stumbling blocks, which hinder you from achieving your enlightened potential, or can be used as the impetus to push yourself forward. It depends on what you do when problems come up.

Some people react to a problem, trying to resolve the problem by other means. This can lead them to feel overwhelmed and forget to use the practice entirely. Then, the obstacle has acted as a stumbling block.

An experienced practitioner has learned to use the practice to take on an obstacle to overcome it. He or she will chant, proactively, with focus and intensity to create a resolution. You can do as they do. When you act in this way, you are using the obstacle as the impetus to impel you forward.

Such obstacles can be subtle and confusing. Here is a list, from the The Soka Gakkai *Dictionary of Buddhism*, so you have some guidelines for recognizing them when they arise:

- Obstacles deriving from earthly desires which arise out of greed, anger and foolishness.
- Obstacles which grow from our negative actions in the past. This can include hindrances from one's spouse or children.
- Past evil actions, resulting in retribution. These hindrances can include opposition from governmental authority or one's parents.
- Obstructions caused by one's physical or mental functions. These hindrances could be physical illness, depression, anxiety or mental illness.
- Troubles arising from earthly desires.
- Fear of one's own death, or doubt caused by someone else's death.
- The tendency to view other human beings as the means to gratify our own wants and wishes or the tendency to submit to someone else who has this view.

According to Nichiren Daishonin, in his writings, you should be neither influenced nor frightened by these obstacles. If you fall under their influence, you could be led into the paths of evil. If you are frightened by them, you can be prevented from practicing.

Let's look at Nancy's situation with Doug. She is encountering more than one of these obstacles. She is living with a person who sees her as someone to satisfy his desires rather than someone who understands she is a person to be respected in her own right. She must also deal with her own training and past. She has learned to let someone else dominate her.

Opposition in the form of these inner and outer workings of life can be subtle and make their detection difficult. The one thing we can be sure of is that obstacles will appear, in the form of our tendencies and weaknesses, to challenge us.

To paraphrase Jude LaClare in the "World Tribune" 12/12/02. You can be confident that you are encountering one of these obstacles if you find yourself becoming passive in your practice, or doubting you have the Buddha nature within. Other indicators include losing the seeking spirit to grow in faith, or becoming critical or cruel to others.

So what should we do when this happens?

- Recommit to the basics of practice and chant for clear goals.
- Try to find opportunities to help others do the same.
- The final step is to look inside of yourself for the cause of your suffering.

You will need to look for tendencies, habits, or weaknesses that are hindering you. The list above gives you a place to start for self-reflection.

When you face obstacles, remember that both inner and outer obstacles are the pathway to enlightenment. As you use the practice to overcome them, first one then another, you will grow in faith and become stronger step by step. After a while you will say as experienced practitioners do, "I don't mind obstacles. They give me something to chant about. I know this is the next step in my growth."

13

Changing Karma

After a couple of hours away, Nancy returned home from the market. Doug had settled down but he held a drink in his hand. Her heart sank. This could mean trouble later, so she resolved to be particularly nice to him. The evening passed without incident, but Nancy felt as though she were walking on eggshells the whole time.

The next morning, she called Hanako from work. She lowered her voice so she wouldn't be heard by her co-workers. "How can I chant at home without setting off fireworks?" she asked.

After a brief silence, Hanako said, "Why don't you come chant at my house today?" They arranged that Nancy would go to her house to chant before going home.

Later on, when Nancy walked into Hanako's living room, she gave a great sigh of relief. She could feel the peacefulness in the room. "It'll feel wonderful to be able to chant without feeling hostile vibes," she said.

"I guess it's really been hard chanting at your house," said Hanako. "After we talked yesterday, you did understand sansho shima didn't you?"

Nancy nodded. "I know I'm supposed to chant, but having him around is very distracting."

"Let's chant about it," said Hanako.

Nancy hadn't thought to chant about it, but she agreed.

They settled down, facing the Gohonzon. Nancy turned to Hanako and said, "Normally I don't know how to speak my feelings with Doug. Yesterday, to my surprise, I just blurted out how I felt. I don't usually say what I really think because he gets angry with me."

Hanako looked pleased. "The fact that you did say something is the beginning of changing your karma."

"What is karma?"

"Karma just means action. Actions can be positive or negative. When we think, say, or do something, we set a seed in our lives which will create an effect at some time in the future, when the conditions are right. Buddhism says that everything in one's environment reflects oneself."

Nancy looked around. Hanako's serenity was mirrored in her home. She had Asian pictures of flowers and bamboo, and the colors she picked for the room were uplifting, just as Hanako herself was. *Hmm, her environment does reflect her.* Aloud, Nancy said, "I guess you're right."

"It's not just a reflection in your house, but in your life circumstances and relationships as well."

"Are you saying this problem with Doug is my fault?" asked Nancy. She'd been afraid of that. Nancy had been raised to think most everything that went wrong was somehow her fault. She cringed inside.

Hanako shook her head. "No, Buddhism doesn't assign fault. We think of our current life situation, our environment, as an expression of our past causes, our karma. Karma also includes life tendencies. I find this principle very heartening. Since we created our circumstances, as they reflect our inner lives, we can change them as well. This is a philosophy of hope, not despair."

Nancy nodded. "So, when obstacles come up, you would say they are due to your karma? And you would say that my relationship with Doug is due to my karma too?"

"Exactly. Part of the practice is changing our karma for the better. You need to value your life. Decide what you want in your life and chant for it."

Nancy looked at the floor, and thought about it for a few moments. "I want a harmonious relationship, a warm home for this coming baby, and a husband who will let me live my life the way I want to. I want us to be partners."

"That sounds pretty clear. I'll chant for that too. Just remember, don't expect it to happen a certain way."

"Okay, that's good to remember. I tend to try to figure out how things will work out." Nancy almost had to laugh thinking of how she'd tiptoed around Doug to keep him from getting angry.

Hanako reassured her. "Most people start out that way. After a few experiences where circumstances work out in surprising ways, you begin to develop the faith that if you just chant, everything will work out somehow."

Nancy remembered some of the stories from the new people's group. She never could have predicted those.

They settled into chairs and faced Hanako's black lacquered carved butsudan. Hanako reached over and flipped a switch to light the Gohonzon. Together they began to chant.

When Hanako sounded the bell to bring the chanting to an end, Nancy commented. "I think I should
chant at home now. If this situation with Doug is part
of my karma, then I want to change that."

Hanako smiled. "You learn quickly."

As she drove home, Nancy reflected on the conversation about karma. Before, she had been a lot more depressed about her life with Doug. Now she had a way
to change their situation. She could feel herself becoming more determined. She didn't know how it would
happen, but she wanted to turn everything around.
She was tired of settling for a life that only pleased others. She was tired of not being happy.

To the Reader

Changing Circumstances From the Inside Out

We discussed oneness of self and environment in a previous chapter. Now, let's deepen this discussion to show how you can change your circumstances.

Western philosophy teaches that everyone is born into an environment separate from them. Buddhism explains that a person and the environment may appear separate on the surface, but both arise from the same source. One cannot exist without the other.

Indeed, Buddhism goes much further and says that each person is born into an individualized environment. There you experience the effects of your past actions, both good and bad. This is your karma, as Hanako discussed with Nancy. The effects of karma appear as your life tendencies, how healthy you are, the shape and structure of your body, your mental states, etc. The effects of your karma also appear in your environment, the parents to whom you come, the conditions in which you live, the circumstances in your country and neighborhood, the people you meet, and the repetitive themes or challenges of your life.

The quality of your environment is determined by who you are internally. The people you attract tend to mirror your inner life. Haven't you known an angry, hostile, person who tends to bring out anger and hostility in the environment around him? And, haven't you known a compassionate person, who creates happiness around him and receives protection and support from others?

This principle becomes more and more subtle as you practice. Ultimately, you come to understand that whatever state of life you manifest will simultaneously manifest in the environment. This means that if you want to change the conditions of your life, the work will have to be done from the inside out.

In the West, without the understanding of the deep connection with our environment, the tendency is to blame people and outer circumstances for our unhappiness. You expect another person to make you happy, or you think if you had more money you would be happy. But Buddhism would say, don't look for the source of your sufferings outside of yourself, either in the environment or in another person.

One example of this was a woman whose husband couldn't be successful in business. He was unwilling to work for anyone else and kept failing repeatedly trying to run his own business. The family was thrown into financial chaos. His wife blamed him for her unhappiness and tried everything she could think of to get him to change. Her situation remained the same.

One day, she decided she didn't have to live with this chaos anymore and took the responsibility for making herself happy, rather than trying to change him. She told him he had three months to find a job. He did nothing, so she left him. As she was earning an income, she and the children became stable financially. The chaos disappeared.

Maybe you have a work or relationship problem in one area of your life where, in the past, you would have blamed the other person. If you address this from the Buddhist perspective, you would chant about it, knowing that this situation reflects something in your life and that you have the power to change it.

When you chant about something or someone, you draw out an infinite wisdom that functions in accord with your changing circumstances. Then you can see the reality of the situation. Experiences which have been obscure come into focus along with the understanding of how to handle them successfully. With this ability comes a great joy that, even within the uncertainty of daily life, you have the resources to handle the circumstances in which you find yourself. To change your circumstances you must change yourself.

14

Steps to Happiness

The district meeting was in full swing when someone knocked at the front door. Nancy was listening as a young man shared an experience about how his temper had disappeared since he started practicing several years before.

One of the women in the back row got up to open the door. "Come on in." She motioned the person on the outside to enter, and opened the door wider.

Doug stood in the doorway. His black hair fell over his forehead in that boyish look Nancy liked. He had his hands firmly in his jeans pockets. Everyone turned to see who was there. When Nancy saw him, she got up to greet him. "Why Doug, I'm glad you came."

"Come out on the porch," he said in a low voice.

"But we're in the middle of the meeting."

"Come on out." He beckoned to her. Nancy stepped out on the porch, leaving the door ajar behind her.

He took her arm. "Come on home with me."

Nancy stepped back. "No, I don't want to leave now. Why don't you come in?"

"Come home with me." Doug's voice got louder and more insistent. His hand pressed her harder.

Nancy stood looking at him confused, not knowing what to say. Inside, she was trembling a bit, unsure of what Doug would do next. Then she became aware that Curt, one of the male leaders, had walked up behind her. Curt stepped around Nancy onto the porch. He looked completely relaxed, his grey eyes warm, as though he didn't realize there was a confrontation going on. "I'm Curt," he said, holding out his hand. "Can I help you?"

Doug looked from Curt to Nancy, ignoring the outstretched hand. "She's my partner and we're leaving now." Nancy knew what he was thinking. His awful jealousy had raised its head again.

Curt looked at Nancy. "Do you want to go?" Nancy shook her head and looked down.

Curt addressed Doug, a firmer edge to his voice but still pleasant. "She doesn't want to go. Why don't you come in and wait for her."

"I don't want to come in. I don't want to be around something that's clearly mind control. Come with me, Nancy." Doug's eyes sparked.

Curt was matter-of-fact yet pleasant. "Nancy has made a decision and she wants to stay. You have to respect her and let her do that."

Doug glared at Curt. Nancy held her breath. She prayed this wouldn't escalate any further.

"You'd be welcome to come in and wait for her." Curt stepped to one side to usher him into the house and Nancy turned around to go back to the meeting. Doug stood alone in the doorway, facing a living room filled with men and women. The whole group looked back. All conversation had stopped. He flushed, looking stubborn. "I don't want to stay, but…" He shrugged and pointed to the hallway. "I'll wait in the next room."

"That's fine." Curt's tone was cordial. "I hope that after the meeting you'll sit and talk with us and find out what we're all about."

Doug didn't answer and hurried into the next room.

Nancy returned to her seat, avoiding everyone's gaze. She'd never been so embarrassed. *How could Doug pull something like this? What would happen when they went home?* Anxiety shot through her.

Hanako patted her arm. "It'll be all right," she whispered. "We'll chant about it." Nancy relaxed a little.

Then, out of the corner of her eye, she saw a couple of the older members, Rob and Scott, leave the room and head in the same direction as Doug. Nancy hoped they were going to talk with him. *I hope he doesn't blow up.* She didn't think he'd been drinking, so maybe he'd stay cool, at least until they were home.

She hated being the center of this kind of attention. At the same time, she was also relieved that someone else besides her could talk with Doug about what she was doing. She felt so unequipped to handle questions. She just didn't have enough experience.

She thought she heard Doug's voice get louder at one point. He seemed to be arguing. She became more anxious. Then the low murmur of voices continued. She was so nervous about what was happening just around the corner that she couldn't pay attention to the meeting. It felt as though she'd sat there for a year before the meeting finally ended.

She was the first one out of her chair and walked hesitantly into the next room. She glanced briefly at Doug.

122

He didn't seem to be angry, but seemed involved with the discussion. "Thanks for waiting for me," she said.

The three men sat around a round teak Scandinavian dining table, the light shining on a bouquet of irises in the center. They glanced up as she entered. Scott with his brown hair, blue eyes, and buttoned-down collar leaned forward, his elbow on the table. He'd clearly been in the middle of an important point. Rob, with his black hair, short-sleeved shirt and jeans, was listening intently.

"We're having an interesting discussion with Doug," Scott said. "He's got some good questions. Why don't you join us?" Nancy took a chair slightly out of the circle. "We were just explaining to Doug that this isn't a social club. It is a practice which allows us to strengthen our lives and become happy."

"It's weird," said Doug. "Nancy's different and I'm not sure I like it."

Rob's deep strong voice enveloped the room. "In what way?"

"She used to spend all her time with me and now she's running off to these meetings and doing this chant at home. And, we're not getting along as well as we were." Doug shifted, looking uncomfortable.

"This is a practice which allows each person to become happy. I'll bet she is chanting for your happiness," said Scott.

Nancy's mouth dropped open. "You're right! I am."

Doug turned to her, a surprised look crossing his face. "Really?"

She found a smile. "Of course. I want you to be happy, and I want to be happy too."

"You think I'll be happy just because you're chant-ing for it? I don't understand that. It sounds like hocus pocus, or magic, or something." Doug smirked.

Rob voice sounded definite. "This isn't magic. You can do an experiment, just like a scientific experiment, and prove this practice to yourself. The reason you become happy is because when you chant, the core of your life, your Buddha nature, responds. One of its characteristics is unshakeable happiness. The more you can enliven that in your life, the happier you will be."

"I've found this practice creates a solid foundation for a marriage," Scott added.

"You think so?" Doug sounded sarcastic and skepti-cal. He folded his arms across his chest and leaned his chair back. "For your information, we've become less happy since she started this chanting." Light glinted on his glasses.

"I don't think so; I know so," Rob said evenly. "I can tell you about one experience after another, where peo-ple who were having trouble overcame it through using the practice. I have a few examples of my own."

Nancy leaned forward, interjecting herself into the conversation, her anxiety not allowing her to remain silent. "I think what's changed is that I am being more true to myself and more honest with you. Don't you want to know how I really feel about things?" Instantly she was sorry she had asked him that.

Doug flushed, then flashed her a look, his eyes turn-ing glacial. "I guess, but you're changing and I liked you the way you were."

Nancy's hopes sank. *Why did I think this was ever go-ing to work? And if it doesn't, then what?*

Rob said, "People do change. But it will always be for the better. The changes Nancy is making are in the direction of her becoming more happy."

"But they aren't making *me* more happy," Doug said hotly.

Nancy braced herself. Here it comes, she thought.

Scott seemed unflappable. "I would suggest that you chant with her. When you do, you'll move in the direction of happiness too, and that will be good for the relationship."

"Me, chant?" Doug was incredulous.

Scott pushed back his chair, got up and left the room for a moment, coming back with a small pamphlet called *The Winning Life* and a card printed with a beautiful lotus flower and the words Nam-myoho-renge-kyo. "You might like to look through this information, so you'll have an idea of what this is."

Rob spoke up. "I'd like to suggest that you pick a goal, something that you want to have happen in your life, and chant for it for ninety days and see what happens. We don't ask anyone to believe something without proving it to themselves. Remember, I said this is a prove-it-to-yourself practice."

"You're not going to ask me to convert then?" A relieved look crossed Doug's face.

Rob smiled. "No. Everyone tries the practice to see whether it fits them, and to find out if they get results. It's like a scientific experiment."

Doug nodded. "What do you mean by results?"

"You'll either get what you chant for, you'll get something better, or you will understand why it is to your benefit you didn't get it. Since you're just beginning, I would chant for something fairly concrete, so you'll know for sure when you get it. Some people have a list of several goals. Or maybe the two of you could chant for a mutual goal. But you can chant for anything you want."

"If you decide to try it, I'd like to be available to you to answer questions or to chant with you," said Rob.

Doug gave Rob an appraising look as though he couldn't believe he'd said that. He seemed both intrigued and conflicted at once.

Doug was debating with himself! Nancy sighed under her breath with relief. At least he hadn't turned down the idea, and looked as though he was actually considering doing it. She wouldn't have believed she'd ever see this.

She returned to the living room to tell Hanako she was going to drive home with Doug. "I think it's okay," Nancy said. "Doug seems to be thinking about trying the practice. The guys were good with him." She hugged Hanako.

Hanako looked up at Nancy. "I hope he does. That sure would solve a lot of problems. I was chanting for him to give it a try while I was waiting for you."

"Keep doing it," said Nancy, chuckling. "I need all the help I can get."

As they drove home, Doug was uncharacteristically silent. Nancy didn't say anything, trying to let him work out whatever he was debating. Finally he said in a grudging tone, "Scott and Rob seemed like okay guys."

Nancy nodded. "One thing about this group that I like is that the men work with the men and the women with the women."

Doug looked at her. "That's a good thing," he said
in a surprised tone.

The drive home was quiet. Nancy was relieved.
Maybe Doug wasn't going to start an argument tonight after all. Maybe this could be the beginning of
something different in their relationship. She hoped
so. In the next few weeks she was going to have to
make some decisions. She still hadn't decided whether
to tell him about the baby or whether she was going
to stay.

To the Reader

Becoming Happy Might Require Change

Now that Nancy has started to chant, her life is changing as she tentatively takes the first steps toward being happy. She's been unhappy, and it's clear that her relationship is going to have to be different for her to become happy. Doug is just beginning to sense the stirrings in the relationship and is acutely uncomfortable with them. He liked the relationship the way it used to be. The future will show whether he can tolerate the necessary adjustments in order for Nancy to become happy and whether those adjustments will allow him to become happy as well.

As long as you are consistently chanting, your life, without doubt, will move in a progressive direction. Even if life as you have known it shifts around you, the purpose is always to move you toward the direction of happiness. Sometimes the necessary changes to move you toward happiness are blocked by existing circumstances. In order for the way to be opened, they must be let go.

One practitioner had been working two part-time jobs and it had been difficult running from one job to the other. Then, without warning, she was laid off by one agency. After the initial shock, she remembered that since she had started chanting, life had been consistently moving her in the direction of happiness. She knew that she had been laid off for something better, and she relaxed. She chanted for the perfect work position. Within a week, it showed up. Her boss in the second agency announced he was leaving, and she was promoted to take his place. It turned out to be a full time position, and she was very happy with it. In fact, in the new job, she had the time of her life.

If Doug can't handle the fact that the relationship must change and ends up leaving, it means that Nancy would never have been able to establish a lasting happiness while living with him. If he decides to begin chanting, any modifications which might occur will also make him happier as well—a win-win solution.

If you have started to chant, you are connected to your Buddha nature, which is one with the evolutionary and eternal life force. Since you are activating it in your life every day, you are more fully connected to its progressive nature. When people aren't practicing, it is as though they have their own life energy but are not fully connected to the greater source. When this is the case, they are more on their own and can become deadlocked. Once you tap into the source every day, you will never again be deadlocked. Chanting daily will enable you to move around or through circumstances which might have stymied you before.

When you are in the depths of a problem, sometimes it's hard to remember that unexpected shifts are always moving you on a progressive path. During these times, it's easy to doubt you have the Buddha nature and you can fall into older, less effective patterns of handling life. When this happens, it's particularly important to stay close to your sponsor and your district, as Nancy is doing, so that more experienced practitioners can remind you what is happening and encourage you.

◢15◣

Tap Into Your Buddha Nature

A week later, on Saturday morning, Nancy had gotten up about nine and had gone to her place in the living room to chant before breakfast. She wanted to develop greater insight about her relationship with Doug. She was getting tired of just doing data entry, so she also chanted about how she might acquire more interesting things to do at work.

She and Doug had not discussed the idea of his chanting since the night of the district meeting. Nancy had decided to leave it alone and let him sort it out for himself. *The Winning Life* lay on the living room coffee table where he'd left it. She was pretty sure he hadn't read it.

As she picked up her beads and faced the wall to begin, Doug walked out of the bedroom. "Don't you feel kind of silly chanting to a blank wall?" he asked.

Did he sound as hostile as before? Nancy flashed back to last week. She didn't think so; he wasn't prowling behind her like he had the other day.

She faced him. "No. I don't feel silly. The Gohonzon just represents what we have inside of ourselves."

"Well it looks silly to me." Doug walked out of the room presumably to get some breakfast. Nancy felt relieved. At least he wasn't as hostile as he had been.

130

She resumed chanting. Her mind began to drift. She wondered how she should handle the subject of the practice with him. She could teach him what Hanako had taught her, about how to set goals and what to do. But he didn't take things from a woman very well, and besides, the group had said that in the practice women teach women and men teach men. Maybe Rob would call him.

Later on that morning the phone rang. A male voice asked for Doug. She handed the phone to him.

"Oh, hi Rob," Nancy heard him exclaim. "You and Scott want to come over here? Why?" A pause. "Oh, okay, two this afternoon."

At two on the dot, the doorbell rang. Doug went to answer it. Scott and Rob stood on the front steps in slickers. She listened to the plop of rain drops on the pathway. It was raining pretty hard. Nancy welcomed them and then went into the kitchen to roll dough to make some biscuits.

She could overhear the conversation in the dining room. She could also see all three men reflected in the dining room's mirror. It was so wonderful having the men chat with Doug. She could hear their low voices as they discussed how to formulate a goal.

Doug commented, "This is very different from meditation. The meditation I did wanted me to get rid of thoughts. You're telling me they're okay?"

Scott asked, "Were you successful in getting rid of the thoughts?"

Doug laughed. "No, I never could stop thinking about things in my life. I finally quit. The same teachers told me that desires were the problem and that we needed to eliminate them. I don't know how you can ever eliminate desires. I couldn't."

Scott smiled and leaned his elbows on the table. "You've hit an important point. Some desires support life, such as the desires for food and shelter. We can't eliminate all of them."

Rob jumped into the conversation. "That's one reason you'll find this practice is quite different from what you've done before." Rob paused. "You'll set goals which may well include things you want. Then you chant for them. If your experience is like mine, obstacles come up whenever you try to achieve something."

Doug agreed reluctantly. "Right. Nothing seems to come easy for me."

Rob gestured with his hands. "Exactly. But instead of giving up or getting angry, we chant to challenge and overcome the obstacle. Sometimes obstacles are internal, such as fears or discouragement. Sometimes they're outward. Whatever they are, if you keep chanting, and don't give up, you will eventually find a way to overcome the obstacle. I promise you."

Doug looked intrigued. "You're saying it's a way to be more successful and to get what I want?"

"You bet," said Scott. "The way I think of it, my Buddha nature is connected to that level of life in all things. When I have an intention it creates an attraction which pulls to me what I need to achieve my goal."

"This sure doesn't sound like any religion I've heard of before."

Scott chuckled. "We think of it more as a way of life. There is a goal for all of us though. We chant to become enlightened and for world peace. We believe that if people are happy, there won't be wars."

There was silence. Nancy continued to roll the dough quietly. She sensed that Doug was thinking about what they were saying.

"I guess that does sound logical."

Scott seized the opportunity. "Why don't we all sit down and chant together?"

Doug didn't answer right away. Nancy prayed that Doug would be willing to try it, but the silence seemed to last forever. Then he said hesitantly, "Okay, I'll try it, but only because you say I can get what I want."

Rob asked, "Do you think Nancy would like to chant with us?"

Doug peeked around the corner at where Nancy stood. "They want to chant with us. Do you want to come in?"

She held up her flour-covered hands and headed for the sink. "Sure, just let me wash up."

In a moment, she had settled into a chair in the dining room, wiping her hands on a dish towel.

Rob turned to Nancy. "We were just discussing how we chant for a goal."

Nancy nodded. "Hanako explained that to me."

Rob turned to Doug. "Trying the experiment is how you'll prove whether this works. You're going to find that life turns into a real adventure."

Rob reached into his pocket and pulled out a small but beautifully decorated wooden box. He slid open the lid, pulled out a small bag, opened it and showed Doug a small plastic box that opened on one side like a book. Inside was a copy of a small scroll, written in Asian-looking characters. Nancy immediately recognized what it was.

Rob explained. "This is a traveling Gohonzon. It's quite small compared to the one you can have in your home." He handed it to Doug to examine. "It's the mandala we focus on while chanting. It represents everything within each of us. It's a mirror of our lives."

Rob pointed to the large letters going down the center from top to bottom. "See Nam-myoho-renge-kyo down the center? That represents your Buddha nature, your enlightened nature that's one with the Mystic Law. When your Buddha nature is enlivened in your life, everything else falls into right order."

Doug shook his head. "Sounds like an idol. I was taught not to pray to idols."

"You're not praying to anything outside yourself. You're tapping into the deepest part of yourself where you already possess unshakeable happiness and a deep wisdom."

Rob turned to Doug and handed him a card with Nam-myoho-renge-kyo written on it. "This is the primary practice. It's called daimoku. Set your intention, your goal, and then begin to repeat Nam-myoho-renge-kyo over and over."

Scott asked them to arrange their chairs so they could focus on the little Gohonzon which he placed on a stack of books. Doug fumbled over the words at the beginning and then appeared to settle into a rhythm. Nancy found it difficult to focus, wondering what Doug was thinking about it all. Then she decided not to worry about it and settled into the chant.

When they ended, Rob reminded Doug of the ninety-day challenge and asked him if he had a goal.

"I guess so. I want to know that my position at work is secure."

"That's a good one," said Scott. "You'll know if you get it. Remember to practice twice each day, morning and evening."

Doug looked very unsure.

Rob spoke up. "I'd like to support you," he said. "Would you be willing to call me once a day and let me know what's going on? I'll read you the daily guidance."

Doug looked a little nonplussed. Nancy held her breath. *How serious was he?* Doug shook his head no. "I don't think I'm ready for that. This whole thing is pretty strange to me. I need more time to think about it."

Rob seemed unfazed by Doug's turn-down. "It's up to you, but you won't be able to tell whether it works by thinking about it. This is an experiential practice. Just remember, either Scott or I will be available if you want to start chanting." They both shook Doug's hand as they got up. Scott and Rob said their goodbyes and left.

To the Reader

Practicing for Self and Others

Not everyone who is introduced to the practice will begin to chant. If you are the family member who has taken up the chant, you might be disappointed by the fact that your significant other or your child doesn't want to start. It is good to know that one person chanting in a family can start the whole family moving into a more progressive direction. It is as though the person who is chanting, through their connection with the Gohonzon, has thrown a protective and progressive mantle over the other family members.

Remember too, that this practice is for oneself and for others. If you are worried about a family member who does not practice, just chant for that person's protection and happiness every day. You can also find out what they want to have happen in their lives and chant for those goals. Any chanting you do for them will give their lives a boost. It would be more powerful if they chanted for their own goals, but you can still help them.

During the formal prayers at the end of *gongyo*, you can chant for people who have died. This is another form of practicing for others and will help assure that their time in between lives and the circumstances for their future lives will be better.

You are always connected with people you care about, even though they may not be physically with you right now.

Chanting for others means to take on their problems as if they were your own, then chanting for them with the same intensity as though you were trying to turn your own problems from poison into medicine. It's always an adventure to see what will happen when you take on another person's problems in this manner.

Another form of practicing for others is to introduce them to Nam-myoho-renge-kyo as Rob, Scott and Hanako have been doing. Part of doing this is teaching to the best of your ability. One of the great joys of introducing another person to the practice is watching as their life turns in a positive direction.

> *"If you light a lantern for another, it will also brighten your own way."*
> Writings of Nichiren Daishonin, p. 1598

> *"Please be confident that the higher your flame of altruistic action burns, the more its light will suffuse your life with happiness. Those who possess an altruistic spirit are the happiest people of all."*
> Daisku Ikeda, *Faith Into Action*, p. 93

⚜16⚜

Why Does This Keep Happening, Anyway?

The next morning Doug raced out the door. He had overslept and was late for work. Although Nancy was disappointed Doug hadn't decided to chant, she resolved to let him find his own way.

Nancy had a more leisurely beginning to her day, since she didn't have to be at work until nine. Settling on the comfortable couch, she found her focal point and chanted for ten minutes. Then she got out the *gongyo* disk and listened to it while trying to pronounce the words. The person on the disc pronounced the words and then repeated them, so she could repeat them after hearing them. She remembered Hanako telling her to try a little each day, so she decided just to focus on three sentences. As she repeated them over and over, listening to the voice on the disc, she gradually got it right.

Later in the afternoon, Nancy returned home first. Doug got home late. He looked worried and tense.

She walked over and put an arm around him. "You look upset, Doug. What's happened?"

"We had four lay-offs today." He paced around the room, running his fingers through his hair.

"Who were they?"

"Various people, I can't see a pattern. Some newer, but some older. It's hard to predict."

"That's nerve wracking."

"You're telling me. But I think I'm okay. I'm doing a good job there."

Nancy didn't believe him. She could see the worry he was trying to hide. She didn't want him to see that she was upset by the prospect. He had enough on his mind. What if he lost his job and then found out she was pregnant too? He might go off the deep end.

She decided to continue her silence about the pregnancy, but she couldn't keep her secret for much longer. Her waistband was getting tighter, and he was going to notice soon.

The uncertainty regarding Doug's job affected Nancy's sleep. She tossed and turned and awoke at four a.m. with tension and fear enveloping her body. What would she do if he lost his job and she had to leave hers because of the baby?

Nancy added another prayer to her chanting session—that Doug and she would be financially stable. She wasn't sure that this would make any difference, but did what Hanako had taught her. Every day when Doug came home, her anxiety rose the moment he opened the door. The days slowly passed and no one else was laid off. She began to hope that the company had stabilized and wouldn't be laying-off anyone else.

Late Friday afternoon, just as she began to relax, Doug slammed open the door. A rush of anxiety and depression came in with him. He was frowning and his eyes looked a little wild.

Nancy reminded herself not to panic. "Doug, what happened?"

Doug started pacing the way he did when he was upset. "I'm going to be laid off in a month! This is exactly what I was afraid of."

Nancy's heart plummeted and her stomach clenched. What were they going to do?

Doug wore an angry expression. "I told you that this Buddhism doesn't work. Haven't you been chanting for me to keep my job?"

"I've been chanting for financial stability."

"What?" His eyes widened. "You mean you haven't been chanting for me to keep my job?"

Nancy didn't want to fight with him. "No. I told you, I'm chanting for our financial stability." She could see he was angling for an argument, so she tried to head it off. "Why not call Rob and see what he says about this?"

But Doug only seemed more agitated. "Why should I?" he said, slamming open and shutting cupboards. "You know what he's going to do. He's going to tell me how great Buddhism is, but look what's happened." Doug pulled out a glass tumbler and filled it with ice.

Nancy was trembling inside, but she picked up the phone and handed it to him. "Please? Do it for me?"

He hesitated, then set down his glass and slowly took the phone from her.

Doug put Rob on speaker phone and quickly explained the situation.

Rob said, "I'm coming over right now."

Fifteen minutes later Rob stepped in and took the lead. "I want all of us to chant about this before we talk.

It's called practicing the Strategy of the Lotus Sutra. When we chant first, we'll have more wisdom when we talk about what's happened."

Doug crossed his arms, and sounded bitter. "This chanting thing doesn't work." He shook his head. "I only called because Nancy wanted me to. I knew this whole thing was too good to be true. Nancy's been chanting for financial stability and now I've been laid off anyway." Doug sounded discouraged. "Some financial stability."

Rob looked directly at Doug and held his gaze. "I know you're feeling like you've been hit with a brick, but this is one of the main reasons we chant, to overcome obstacles in life. I would suspect that maybe this company couldn't give you job security and so, in order to have it, you might have to work somewhere else."

Doug seemed to be considering Rob's words. Finally he said, "I hadn't thought of that." He seemed to be remembering something. "Or maybe I did," Doug exclaimed. He turned to Nancy. "Didn't I tell you that I thought people were going to be laid off?"

Nancy nodded.

Doug looked at the floor. "I just didn't think it would be me."

Rob held up a hand. "Believe me this isn't the first time I have seen something like this happen," he said. "I know you haven't really made a decision to chant, but I hope you'll try the experiment. The practice is much more powerful when you are chanting for your own issues."

Doug hesitated. Nancy could see him battling with himself. She also knew he didn't know what else to do to handle the layoff.

Doug looked up, a faint glint of hope in his eyes. "You really think it can make the difference?"

"Absolutely," said Rob, radiating confidence. "I have seen one person after another come up against something like this and have it work out for the best."

"Give me an example."

"One person was three months behind in rent when she started the practice. She started chanting, and taking one step after another, her life began to turn around. District members helped her get her computer working, so she could do her online jewelry business. Someone built her a supply case so she could show her jewelry at a flower store. The owner of the store got her started selling flowers on the street and then gave her a thirty-two hour a week job. She was delighted and came up to me and said, 'Now I can really live again."

Doug looked skeptical. "How do you know it was the chanting?" He demanded. "How do you really know?"

Rob spoke directly to him. "I'll tell you what I know from experience, Doug. When people chant, their lives start to move forward and difficult things work out." He paused. "If you watched someone drop an apple off a roof once, you might not think there was any particular reason for it. But if it happened, twenty or fifty or one hundred times, wouldn't you begin to think there was something that made that apple fall the same way every time?"

Doug shrugged. "Probably."

"Well, it's just like that with the chant. I've been doing this for twenty-five years and have heard one experience after another. When people have chanted about the difficulties in their lives, they've landed on their

142

feet, and their lives became better than before. What are you afraid of about this?"

Doug's shoulders went back and he bristled, sticking out his chin in a pugnacious stance. Nancy held her breath. *Please don't get nasty.*

Emphatically, Doug blustered, "I'm not afraid of anything."

"Good, because chanting about this layoff doesn't commit you to anything. It's an experiment to see whether the practice works."

"I think it's crazy." Doug's bravado deflated. "But I don't know what else to do."

"You'll try it then?"

Doug hesitated and then nodded slowly. "I guess, even if it's just to prove to you that it doesn't work."

Rob's laughter crinkled the skin around his eyes. He looked genuinely amused. "People have tried just that and are still doing the chant thirty years later. You won't regret it. Now, let's talk about how to chant for a goal. Okay?"

Rob nodded.

"Keep your goal in mind, seeing it as having already completed. Keep your thoughts on your goal, not on your fears. Then chant hard to achieve your goal."

Doug nodded slowly.

"You're lucky you didn't have to leave the company today. That's actually a benefit because you'll have time to work with the practice on your situation." He turned to Nancy. "Good for you. To some degree your chanting has actually protected Doug."

Rob opened his burgundy briefcase. Nancy had wondered what was in it. He pulled out a blue and white book, *Faith into Action*, and flipped through the pages. He pointed to a page. "Read this."

> *"When your determination changes, everything will begin to move in the direction you desire. The moment you resolve to be victorious, every nerve and fiber in your being will immediately orient itself toward your success. On the other hand, if you think, 'This is never going to work out,' then at that instant every cell in your being will be deflated and give up the fight. Then everything really will move in the direction of failure."*
> Daisaku Ikeda, *Faith into action*, p. 108

Doug raised his hands defensively. "That's not so easy."

Rob's voice was soothing. "I know, but all of us men will be chanting with you to support you till you get through to the other side."

"You would do that for me?" Doug's eyebrows went up, skepticism evident. "No one even knows me." Nancy remembered that Doug had never really had male friends.

Rob smiled, his eyes kind. "Of course. You've started chanting which makes you one of the group. This is part of the great value of the organization: you aren't out there by yourself. Now, I need to ask you some hard questions to decide how we should chant. Is this the first time you've been laid off?"

Doug looked away. "Unfortunately not," he said almost inaudibly. "It's happened two other times." He looked as though he wanted to sink through the floor. Nancy was shocked. She hadn't known this.

Rob was undaunted. "Even though it may feel that way, it's not the end of the world. The Buddhist point of view is everything that happens in our lives is the result of past karma or action. When you see a repetitive circumstance you can bet on it. One of the important things about this practice is that we *can* change our karma."

"I don't know why this keeps happening." Doug looked lost, bewildered, as though he was subject to forces he didn't understand. Nancy felt a rush of sympathy for him and then, right on its heels, an equal rush of anger. *How could he hide this from me? What else might he have hidden?*

Rob continued. "This whole situation provides you with an opportunity to get through this karma so you don't have to keep experiencing it. You'll want to chant to understand the root cause of why this keeps happening." Rob held up a warning hand as Doug started to speak, "And, you should chant for your employer's happiness."

Doug's mouth dropped open. "What! Why? I'm furious with him right now."

Rob's voice remained even. "Remember, any situation in our lives is the effect of our own past actions and is not the fault of anyone else."

Doug's eyes flashing, he stood up abruptly, almost knocking over the chair. "You're blaming me?"

Rob looked up at Doug and remained seated. He wasn't put off by Doug, Nancy thought.

"No point in getting angry. I'm not blaming you. I'm asking you to understand that it's a law, like gravity. Even if we haven't heard of gravity, if we step off a high building we'll fall. Would you blame someone who'd never heard about gravity and fell off a building?"

"I guess not," Doug said reluctantly, sitting back down. He tipped back his chair like a school boy and looked down his nose at Rob. Nancy hoped it wouldn't fall over or the chair's legs break. The rungs had gotten looser because of his childish habit.

Rob flashed him a smile, paying no attention to Doug's upset. He leaned forward with some intensity. "Fortunately, with the practice, we can make this law work in our favor rather than unconsciously end up with consequences we haven't anticipated. I want you to add something else to the experiment."

"Something *else*?" Doug's chin came out again.

Rob persisted. "No matter how you feel, I want you to be the best employee your boss has ever had for the next four weeks. That means pay attention to every detail."

Doug scowled. "Wow, you don't want me to do much do you?"

"You're not going to like it, but you have to remember that all of our life circumstances come from the inside out." Doug started to protest but Rob just continued in a pleasant tone. "That fact gives us a great opportunity because, if we created it, we can change it."

Doug sat back looking half-angry and half-thoughtful. Nancy held her breath. At least he hadn't blown up, or maybe it was that Rob just hadn't let him. She saw that when someone didn't just give in to Doug, he at least listened.

Rob asked, "Do you want to get through this successfully? If so, you'll have to spend some real time chanting."

"Like how much time?"

"Until you feel as though the problem is resolved. Sometimes when there is a serious problem, people chant for long periods of time."

Doug's defiance suddenly collapsed. His shoulders slumped. "You think I can really get through this?"

Rob radiated confidence. "I know it. Absolutely."

With that, Doug straightened up. A look of determination came into his eyes. "Okay then. Show me how to do it."

Rob sat down beside Doug and asked him to face the wall and pick a focal point. "Chanting about something before strategizing about it is called practicing the strategy of the Lotus Sutra," Rob said. "You have much deeper wisdom when thinking about the issue after chanting."

Then Rob repeated Nam-myoho-renge-kyo slowly and then more and more quickly. Doug followed him, at first seeming to stumble over the words. As Rob picked up the speed, Doug seemed to follow him quite well.

Rob turned to Nancy. "I'd like you to join us. The more people who chant to support another person, the better. Let's chant for Doug to have a stable job which he enjoys and fits his skills. Okay Doug?"

Doug nodded. "That sounds good."

"When you pick a goal, make sure it is a determination and not just a hope. A determination means that you are going to do whatever is necessary."

"Even if I don't know what to do?"

"Yes, as time goes on that will come to you." Rob pulled out his little Gohonzon and set it on the table. Rob led the three of them in chanting for half an hour. Nancy felt a great relief. They had something more than just their own abilities to deal with this situation. Seeing Rob's confidence and knowing they were supported by the group really helped her.

When they finished the room felt calm.

Rob turned to Doug and asked him what he had experienced.

"I had a lot of thoughts."

"That's right, you will," said Rob. "Any thoughts about your job situation?"

"I'm not sure I want to talk about that," Doug said. "Some of them are private."

"That's fine," said Rob. "If you learned anything about actions you can take to deal with the situation or to change something you are doing, then I would try to take those actions. We can learn a lot about ourselves when we chant, and we don't always like what we see."

Nancy reflected on what she had heard at the district meeting. "I heard Clint say he has a list he is still working on after twenty years."

Rob smiled. "I've had to make a lot of changes myself." He turned back to Doug. "It's important that you chant until you achieve your goal. Don't even try to predict how it will come about. Sometimes you can't even imagine how you might get your goal."

Doug nodded. "I'll try, but it seems really strange."

"Of course it does. You're trying something new and I'm asking you to do something which is contrary to your training."

Nancy watched the whole interchange with amazement. She had never seen men talk about themselves as readily as these men did. Who would have thought her quick-tempered boyfriend, who rarely looked at his responsibility in a situation, would have responded like this to Rob?

Hanako hadn't explained karma this way to her. She had told her she would have to change herself. Rob had told Doug that if he wanted to overcome his karma he should be the best employee his boss had ever had, which amounted to the same thing, but was less direct. Maybe she could learn something from Rob's approach.

It wasn't going to be just the men who chanted for Doug. She would ask Hanako to chant with her about this too. She became inwardly determined. They were going to turn poison into medicine. Somehow this was going to work out.

To the Reader

Understanding the Simultaneity of Cause and Effect

In Buddhism, there is a concept called the simultaneity of cause and effect. This means that with every thought, word, or action, you are setting a seed deep in your life which will manifest at some time in the future. The current action creates the seed. Karma is the manifestation of that seed at some time in the future, when the conditions are right. In other words, our destiny is created through our actions. For example, a child who practices the scales on the piano grows up to be a piano player. A person who eats too much becomes overweight.

Karma basically just means action and can be either negative or positive. It appears in our lives both as events, as well as habitual actions.

Doug was let go from three different places of work. Undoubtedly, he demonstrated behaviors which contributed to his being laid off, rather than his lay-off being a matter of someone else being chosen over him. For example, he had a habit of rapidly getting angry, and he didn't like to take responsibility for mistakes. These habits probably didn't help Doug in the workplace either.

Abilities and interests can be examples of karma as well. These might include being very adept at one thing or another, for example having musical versus scientific interests.

When you see a recurring pattern in your life you can be sure you are dealing with some karmic issue. A positive example might be a person who appears to have been born with a lucky gene. Everything seems to work out for that person, they are in the right place at the right time. Some people just seem to always have wonderful, loyal friends.

Some negative examples might include being chronically overweight, being fired repeatedly, or having an addiction. The practice allows us to address the negative tendencies in our lives, and strengthen the positive ones.

The steps to changing negative patterns are seen in the way Rob worked with Doug.

We created the circumstances in our lives and we have the power to change them. The point of power resides in each of us at any given moment.

Overcoming our negative tendencies, or fundamental darkness, is the way that practitioners work to transform their lives. If you put these steps into practice with a problem facing you, you can overcome your own life tendencies as well. Overcoming one challenge after another not only places your life firmly on an upward trajectory, it also increases your faith and ultimately allows you to establish unshakeable happiness in the core of your life.

Of course when you are faced with a major challenge, it is possible to become discouraged or develop doubt that you will be able to overcome the obstacle. It's important at that time to stay close to other practitioners who will give you support while you go through the difficult period.

Remember the discussion on oneness of self and environment? When in the trenches, recall that events in your life manifest from the inside out. This means you have created your circumstances. If you try to solve your problem by trying to change or blame someone else, you have given your power away. Since you had the power to create the circumstance, you have the power to change it. But to change your circumstances you must change yourself. Buddhism teaches that as you make inner shifts, everything in your outer situation will shift as well.

An example of how this works can be seen in the following experience. One practitioner had lived a lifetime feeling as though she were an outsider. She never felt part of any group with whom she socialized. On a new job, the same pattern persisted. She felt like an outsider there as well.

Having started to practice, she came to understand that if she wanted this situation to change, she would have to change the way she related to her co-workers. Instead of holding herself somewhat aloof, preoccupied with her own concerns, she reached out to them, making a point of greeting them in the morning and asking about their lives. Her co-workers responded and she found herself included in the group.

The problems you encounter would have occurred whether you were chanting or not. With the practice you have a way of overcoming them successfully.

17

Twists and Turns: Never Give Up

After Rob had closed the door behind him, Doug turned on Nancy with eyes flashing, "I told you I didn't really believe in this. I'm doing it for you, just to prove to you it doesn't work. I don't like to talk to people about what is going on in my life."

Nancy startled, involuntarily took a step backwards and then reached inside herself for courage. "I know. But this job situation is such a big thing. And what if it does work? If it doesn't, we're no worse off than we are now. But if it does, we're so much better. What do you have to lose?"

Doug backed off. "I guess you're right about that."

Nancy persisted. "I really hope you'll do the other things Rob suggested."

Doug gave her a wry smile. "If it doesn't work and I haven't really given it an honest effort, I'll never hear the end of it."

Nancy had to chuckle. That was true. She was surprised to hear Doug talk about giving work an honest effort. She hadn't heard him talk that way before. He didn't tend to put a lot of himself into work.

Doug wasn't the only one who had to think about job issues. She had realized as Rob was talking that she had her own karma to deal with. She didn't know how to speak up for herself and, if she didn't get over the fear of doing that, she could be stuck as an administrative assistant for a long time.

This could be a problem. If she decided not to stay with Doug, she was going to have to have a job that would support both her and the baby. She certainly wasn't making enough to do that now. She decided that she would make that one of her goals, to find a better job, either at the agency or somewhere else where she could support herself, regardless of whether she stayed with Doug or not.

For the next month, Nancy focused her chanting time around two goals, being able to speak up for herself and finding a job that could support her and the baby. She found she was chanting for longer periods. One Monday morning, after she finished, she realized that she was becoming more confident about the things she needed to do.

When she got to work that day, she asked Lisa if she would walk with her during break. The two young women stepped outside. Nancy appreciated the fresh air. It was so refreshing after the tired air in the agency. Suffering drains the life out of the air, she thought.

They started down the pathway, enjoying the mallard ducks and their babies paddling in the stream next to the bike path.

Nancy knew she could trust Lisa and tell her what was going on. She said, "Doug has been told he will be laid off at the end of the month."

Lisa seemed genuinely concerned. "I'm so sorry," she said. "You don't need this right now."

Nancy nodded. "I've been chanting a lot to turn this around," she said. "Are you chanting?"

Lisa brightened. "I sure am. I've settled down more in my job; I'm not so restless." Lisa smiled at Nancy. "Chanting has made me appreciate that I have a steady job and a decent work environment. Before, I'd never been good at appreciating anything." They walked in companionable silence for a few minutes.

Then Lisa turned to Nancy. "How's the ninety-day challenge going? What does Doug think of it?"

Nancy sighed. "At the beginning he wasn't happy about my chanting. It was a hassle, and we fought when I wanted to go to the meetings. Now that he's been told he's going to be laid off, I asked him to call Rob. Rob has encouraged him to experiment with the practice around this job situation."

Lisa's dark eyebrows raised in a surprised, questioning look. "Really? Doug said he'd try chanting?"

"He didn't really want to do it, and told me he's trying it just to prove to me it doesn't work. But he's actually been chanting." Nancy shook her head in amazement.

Lisa's eyes danced. "I'd say that's your first benefit."

Nancy realized Lisa was right. "I guess so," she agreed. Hmm. She hadn't thought of it that way.

"Have you told him about the baby?"

"No, I want to see how we're getting along. I have about six weeks before I'll have to tell him."

Lisa looked her up and down. "You don't show yet. That would put you third month?"

Nancy nodded. "I'm hoping I won't grow my baby bump right away. I'm tired a lot though." She pointed to the baby ducklings. "How old do you think they are? They're so sweet."

Lisa glanced in their direction. "I would imagine just a few days." She looked at Nancy. "You know, I've noticed something. You haven't been running to the bathroom and crying like you were for a while."

Nancy smiled. "That's true. I made a decision I didn't want to look like an incompetent idiot and jeopardize my job."

"That's great!" Lisa exclaimed. "I'm so glad. I hadn't wanted to tell you that Annette's been seriously unhappy. I was afraid for you."

"Well, I decided to change that." Nancy felt more determined than she had in years, but hearing of Annette's concern, fear crept back into her thoughts. "Was she talking about me in the office?" Nancy felt embarrassed. Who else knew what Annette thought?

"I overhear her when she talks on the phone. I haven't heard her say anything for a while, though."

"That's a relief." Nancy looked at her watch. "Time to go back."

◆

Doug was having a harder time. He decided to set his focal point in the bedroom where he could close the door. He didn't want Nancy or anyone else watching him while he chanted.

The first time he sat down to try chanting, he took a deep breath. He felt like an idiot. But he'd said he'd do this chant for ninety days. He got out a pen and paper and wrote down this goal: A job that uses my abilities, is secure, and that I like.

Even though he had a goal, he didn't really believe it could happen. He felt resistant and seriously questioned why he was doing this at all.

He went to work the next day. He had chanted at home and had felt better when he finished, but when he walked into his office he got angry all over again. He just couldn't believe that George had laid him off. Maybe he didn't always give a hundred and ten percent but he'd done an adequate job. He was sure of that.

In spite of his best intentions, he snapped at people in the office that first week. This whole situation was so unfair. He hadn't done anything to deserve this.

He became aware during his chanting time that his temper wasn't helping him in the work situation. The people around him were avoiding him.

His inclination was to just brush it off. Why should he care? They were just going to let him go anyway. But then as he continued to chant he thought, my temper hasn't helped me before. Maybe I should try to do something different. He remembered Rob saying he wanted him to be the best employee he could possibly be. He hadn't really been trying very hard, he had to admit. He ended the chanting session with the resolve to try harder.

Battling against himself, he tried to put a cap on his temper at work. It wasn't easy. He had to bite his tongue more than once. He felt like a wimp.

Rob called. "How are things going with the chanting and work?" he asked.

Reluctantly, Doug explained. "I'm trying hard to keep my temper. I feel like a wimp, though." He still hated having to talk about his life.

Rob was upbeat as usual. "I don't think you're being a wimp at all. I'd say that's progress. You're getting stronger."

"What do you mean stronger?" Doug demanded. He'd always thought that being strong meant that you controlled the situation. He'd always done that by being angry. People were intimidated by him. He felt a secret satisfaction at the thought.

"Men who can't control their emotions are weak," Rob said matter-of-factly. "The ones who can are strong, because they can handle any circumstance without going out of control. Losing your temper just gives the other person the advantage."

That comment hit Doug like a brick. *Other men thought that?* He got off the phone quickly. He remembered that Rob hadn't gotten angry in their first discussions, when he could have. This had given Doug the feeling he could say what he thought.

That night as he chanted, memories of times when he'd become angry came to him. He saw he'd intimidated some people but others had used his temper to their advantage. He thought of Nancy. His temper had hurt their relationship, particularly when he'd gone out of control and put the hole in the wall. He cringed inside. He didn't really want to know what she thought of that now. He had to wonder if Rob could be right. He might be. He'd try harder to control his temper at work and see what happened.

The next day, his secretary Marcy came into Doug's office. "Mr. McClure, what should I do about the Smith account? They're two months overdue." What a stupid question, Doug thought, anger rising. He started to snap at her, but then controlled himself. "I'll show you the protocol," he told her instead.

That night, while chanting, he thought of his father. He had a temper of his own. Doug had looked up to his father, but had been afraid of him too. He never knew when his dad would explode and hit someone. Then the question came. *Do I want people to be afraid of me?* He shifted uneasily in his chair.

Memories continued to come to him. *I didn't tell Dad things that were important to me, or go to him when I was afraid, or when I got into trouble at school. I was afraid he'd blow up. Mother would act scared and go in her room and cry.*

More than once she'd taken him and stayed at his grandmother's for a few days. He had worried she would never go back. Is this what he wanted for himself with Nancy? No, he thought determinedly. He wanted things to be better in his family. He felt discouraged. He'd had a temper for so long! Could he really get a handle on it?

Rob called again. "Hi Doug, how are things going?"

Doug mumbled, "Okay." He didn't want to tell Rob how hard it was.

"I'd like to invite you to a new people's meeting," Rob said.

Doug's first reaction was that he didn't want to go. Then he remembered he'd committed to do this for ninety days. "I'll come," he said reluctantly.

Doug slid into a chair at the newcomer's meeting. After *gongyo,* Scott announced the topic. "Tonight we're going to discuss how to handle obstacles to achieving goals." He threw the question out to the group. "Has anyone had an experience where you set a goal and ran into obstacles to achieving it? If so, how did you use the practice to handle it?"

160

Hanako raised her hand. "I've had an experience." Scott nodded encouragement. Hanako said, "My husband and I were going to move out of state to take care of his aging parents. I'd noticed some physical symptoms of my own but was very busy with my job and getting ready to move, so I didn't go to the doctor right away.

Finally, after I closed down my job, I went to the doctor. He took one look at me and did a biopsy at once. My husband returned from out of state and the day before we were due to leave, my doctor told me I had cancer and needed to deal with it right away."

Scott asked, "How did you handle it?"

Doug listened intently. He couldn't imagine what he would have done in a situation like that.

"My husband was very upset, but I really wasn't," said Hanako. "I'd been practicing almost forty years and had seen one person after another overcome cancer, financial problems, every kind of problem you can imagine. I knew I just had to sit down once we got to Oregon and start some serious chanting about it. That turned out to be three hours a day, once we arrived."

So that's what Rob meant when he said I might have to chant more, thought Doug. "Whew! That's a lot of time chanting," he said aloud.

"It certainly is," Scott said, "but when you're faced with something like cancer you're dealing with a very serious problem. Most problems don't require that kind of time."

Hanako continued. "That was just the start of the problems," she said, looking around at the group. "We didn't have insurance here that any doctor wanted to take. So we had to chant hard about that. Finally, after about five weeks, I was referred to a good oncologist, one of the few who would take our insurance. I had the surgery." She gave the victory sign. "I've been cancer-free for four years." Everyone clapped.

Scott asked, "Did you ever get discouraged?"

Hanako paused briefly. "Yes, it was a challenge for sure, but if I'd given up in the middle, I wouldn't have achieved my goal."

Doug thought about it. "So, if you have a goal you have to keep chanting until you get it? That's what you mean?"

"Exactly," Scott said.

As Doug sat there he began to see a small point of light in the dark tunnel of his life. *These people really thought a person could overcome problems with the chanting and change their lives.* When he went home he felt oddly comforted, as though he wasn't alone with this job situation. That evening, he felt a little more relaxed.

Even though he had felt supported at the meeting, the actual work day didn't become any easier. Doug continued to struggle to be a better employee. He stopped putting off projects until the last minute. Instead, he paid particular attention to the work he was doing and volunteered to do extra projects. One day, a couple of weeks later, he realized that it was getting easier to keep a handle on his temper. When he felt like blowing up he just didn't say anything.

But Doug felt embarrassed when his secretary commented, "You seem happier recently." *Of course she didn't know what was going on, but she'd noticed. I wonder who else notices what I do?*

While chanting that evening, a thought came to him. Maybe he'd been laid off for something more than economics. He'd been doing his best for the last three weeks. Had his extra effort made a difference with his boss? He probably should talk with him. A rush of anxious feelings followed on the heels of that thought. Then he remembered Rob saying, "Just chant and don't worry about how it's going to happen." Doug decided not to talk with George, but to just continue doing what he had been doing.

The day, before his last day of employment, George asked him to come to his office. Doug knocked on the door and his boss waved him in. He sat down on a straight-backed chair by the end of the desk.

George looked at Doug over the top of his steepled fingers. His boss looked tired and stressed and had developed bags under his eyes. Doug wondered why he looked so tired but didn't think he should ask.

Finally George spoke. "What's been going on with you for the last three weeks?"

Doug hesitated. He didn't want to talk about the chanting. Then taking a deep breath, he said, "I understood I needed to change what I was doing here." He looked at the floor.

George nodded in agreement. "You have. From what I've seen, your temper has improved a lot, you've been thorough in your duties and you've volunteered to fill in where needed. I appreciate the effort you've made. Your temper and inattention to work were problems for people working with you."

Shocked and embarrassed, Doug nodded. He hadn't realized that's how George saw him. Suddenly, Doug realized he'd held his job this last year by a hair.

George continued. "Unfortunately, even though you've made a real effort, the layoff is due to the economy, so I'm afraid tomorrow will be your last day. I hope you won't be discouraged by this but will give your next employer the kind of work you have given us for the last three weeks. The kind of effort you've been making recently can only be to your benefit anywhere you go."

Doug flushed. He'd so hoped that George would have changed his mind. He nodded that he understood. "Would you give me a letter of recommendation?"

George briefly hesitated and then said, "Based on the changes you have made in the last three weeks, I'll be happy to have it ready for you by the end of the day."

Doug nodded, "Thanks. I'd better go and clean out my desk."

As he walked back to his office, Doug wrestled with conflicting emotions. He was stunned at how close he'd come to being fired while working there. He felt angry he had been laid off, while other employees kept their jobs. Still, George's comments about Doug's recent efforts warmed him. It'd been a long time since he'd had such positive feedback.

Doug thought about his experiment with chanting. Obviously, it hadn't worked. If it had, he wouldn't have been laid off. He felt duped. As he climbed into his car his anger took over. Nancy and those chanters had played him for the fool. He'd had so much hope that chanting would work. Not only had the chanting failed, now he was disappointed too. He peeled out of the parking lot. Just wait until he talked to Nancy.

To the Reader

Chanting for as Long as It Takes

As Doug has just discovered, there may be unexpected twists and turns when chanting for a goal. Sometimes when you chant for a goal, you run into circumstances where you appear to be blocked from achieving your goal. This might be the time when doubts assail you and the goal seems impossible. You might even be tempted to give up.

These doubts are your fundamental darkness, which obscures the fact that you have that connection to the Mystic Law of Nam-myoho-renge-kyo, and have the capacity to create your life as you wish it.

Experienced practitioners know that the middle stages of chanting for a goal are often frustrating and difficult. They have experienced many times that, if they persist chanting for their goal, despite the difficulties, they have gotten their goal or something better. On the rare occasion when they haven't achieved the goal, they have seen why it was to their benefit.

Twists and turns may be necessary for your goal to finally materialize. Doug is chanting for a secure job which fits his abilities. We know that his company is in the throes of financial difficulties and that is why he is being laid off. It may be impossible for him to have a secure job in a company which is experiencing financial issues. In this case, his being laid off might actually represent a step forward toward his goal of having a secure position. Of course, he doesn't understand this yet.

If you are in the frustrating situation of chanting for a goal and not appearing to be making movement forward, it will be important to examine how you are chanting. Are you of two minds about your goal? If so, you will not have a good result. You need to be clear on what you really want. If you continue to be unsure, you might want to chant for clarity.

Are you chanting to get out of something you *don't* want? Or, are you chanting for what you *do* want? It's important to always chant for the result you do want.

Are you chanting with a hope, but not really believing you can achieve your goal? Or, are you chanting with a determination that you will achieve this goal and are willing to do whatever is necessary to bring it about? Hope alone will not bring results.

You must chant with determination for what you wish to happen in your life. If you are immersed in doubts, they become your prayer to the universe. Remember oneness of self and environment? Our environment reflects what we are. Just look at the end result—what you want—and rein in those doubts.

Fortunately, you don't have to know or control how your goal will come about. Sometimes the hardest part of the process is letting go of the wish to control. If you continue to chant, you will find through repeated experiences that you don't have to control the process. Your goals will materialize in ways you could never imagine. After a while you will come to trust that the universe will work out the path. All you must do is move forward, one step at a time.

You don't have to chant obsessively about a goal. But you do need to set up your intention and the determination you aren't going to give up until you get it. The universe knows what you need and want. Even though it may take time for all the pieces of your goal to pull together, if you chant and consistently take action on the ideas that come to you, it will come to fruition.

This is why, when experienced practitioners hit the middle stages of chanting for a goal, they gear in for as long as necessary. They know if they just persist, the best result is assured. We saw that spirit demonstrated in Hanako's experience. So just hang in there, don't be discouraged, and never give up.

> *"Though one might point at the earth and miss it, though one might bind up the sky, though the tides might cease to ebb and flow and the sun rise in the west, it could never come about that the prayers of the practitioner of the Lotus Sutra would go unanswered."*
>
> *Writings of Nichiren Daishonin*, p. 345

When doubts come up, as they certainly will, that's the time to get support from other, more experienced members of your group. They will chant with you, and remind you first, that obstacles are the path, and second, if you just hang in there, you possess everything you need to overcome the obstacle. Most of all, they will encourage you never to give up until you reach your goal.

18

Benefits and Self Knowledge

The moment Doug stepped into their apartment, Nancy knew. Without a doubt, he had lost his job.

"Nancy?" called Doug. He swung around to where she sat on the couch. He threw his raincoat onto a chair and ran his fingers through his hair. He looked white around the mouth as though he'd had a shock. He also looked angry.

He sounded outraged. "George laid me off anyway, even after all the effort I've made!" He stood looking at her accusingly, his hands on his hips.

Nancy panicked. Suddenly there didn't seem to be enough oxygen in the room. She tried to regain her internal balance. "He really laid you off?" She put her hand on her belly. Because of the baby, Doug's job loss could be more serious than it might have been otherwise. How would they cope? Thank goodness they had her income. But how long would she be able to stay on the job? *No point in getting so upset.*

Doug sank down slowly onto a dining room chair, his shoulders hunched over like an old man's. "George recognized the effort I've been making the last three weeks but he still couldn't keep me on. He said it was because of the slow-down in sales."

She struggled to center herself. Her breathing slowed. "I'm glad at least he recognized that you're trying." She considered for a moment. "Did he give you a letter of recommendation?"

Doug nodded. "Yes, thank goodness."

"That's wonderful." She went over to him, laid her cheek on the top of his head. She loved his thick dark hair and that it smelt like shampoo. She kissed his hair. "You really weren't fired, you know. He would have kept you if he could have." He leaned into her for a moment and put his arms around her waist. Then he straightened up.

"My head knows that but it's not much comfort. I don't know what we're going to do."

Nancy braced her back. "I still have a job, so we aren't going to be out on the street. That gives you time to look. We should chant about this and see what comes up." Doug didn't respond.

She remembered how Rob had formulated the goal when they chanted for Doug's job opportunity. "Weren't you chanting for a secure position that fit your abilities?"

"Yes."

"That's different from chanting for this particular job."

Doug's lips curled into a sneer, "come on Nancy. Just face it. Chanting doesn't work. I've just proved it to you."

She took a deep breath determined not to be bullied. "No, you haven't."

Doug looked surprised but he didn't say anything. "You were chanting for a secure position. That might not be with this company."

"Give it up!" Doug's voice rose and his cheeks flushed. "I don't want to hear any more about chanting. I tried it and it didn't work. Period."

Nancy could see that he felt discouraged, and that he was hurting too much to listen right now. She didn't want to trigger his temper either. She was too tired to deal with it, so she let it go. For now.

Doug stood up and headed for the kitchen. A moment later she heard the clink of ice cubes. She knew what that meant. Life wasn't going well for him so he was going to drink and zone out to kill the pain. Instead of dealing with his problems, he was drinking more and more. She was worried.

She headed to the bedroom to chant. If he heard her she was afraid it would be like throwing gas on a fire. She didn't want to fight with him—especially when he'd been drinking. On the other hand, she needed to chant to produce a positive outcome. She couldn't give up because Doug might be angry. She closed the door and chanted quietly for twenty minutes.

She got up to prepare dinner and passed Doug, still sitting in the recliner. "How would you like fried chicken and mashed garlic potatoes tonight?" she asked.

He glanced up from watching the news. More bombings in the Middle East. "That would be great." Nancy didn't know how he could watch all that negativity. Particularly now, when his own life had hit the skids.

As she whisked the potatoes she reflected on how Doug must be feeling. With his history of losing jobs, this must be a double blow. He could use the support of the men in the organization. Even though he was upset right now, he always seemed more optimistic after they left.

She resolved to call Rob after Doug fell asleep. When he sat drinking in front of the television, he tended to doze off. If Doug stayed awake, she'd call Rob tomorrow. She'd ask him to touch base with Doug and leave her out of it.

Doubts she'd felt earlier, that the chant might not work, resurfaced. Why hadn't Doug been able to keep his job? She'd have to talk it over with Hanako as soon as possible.

To the Reader

Realizing Earthly Desires Can Lead to an Awakening

Both Doug and Nancy are experiencing an illusion common to beginners in the practice. They think that the proof of the chant is whether they get what they are chanting for—a specific benefit.

Remember the ten worlds? In terms of the ten worlds, chanting for a specific benefit amounts to chanting for gratification, or the world of rapture. Practitioners often receive benefits of this kind.

But sometimes the benefit you receive leads to awakening, rather than to immediate gratification.

Let's look at some examples. One young woman started chanting during the hippie days of the 1960s. She chanted for marijuana and she received some. She had chanted for an hour and her life condition was high before she decided to smoke the marijuana. When she smoked it, the drug brought her down. After a couple more experiences like that, she gave up marijuana entirely. Her experience had led to an awakening.

In another example, two practitioners, a husband and wife were in the process of remodeling a fixer-upper house with a gorgeous river view. In the middle of the process the wife realized they didn't have enough money to complete the remodel. They had a construction loan which required they complete all the projects on the loan.

If they didn't complete them in a timely manner, they could lose the house.

Faced with this situation, the wife started chanting for money to complete the house. They needed twenty-five thousand dollars and couldn't borrow any more money from the bank. They didn't have any other resources. She told no one she was chanting for the money.

About three weeks later, her sister called and asked if she could use a loan of five thousand dollars. She accepted gratefully, planning to use it on wall board and wiring. She had chanted for another month when her brother called and said he wanted to invest some trust money in real estate. Could she use twenty thousand dollars? This gave them the resources they needed to complete the work on the house.

Although she received the benefit, the real awakening lay in the realization that she had a Buddha nature and could manifest whatever was needed from the universe. She realized she didn't have to worry about money any longer.

Let's take a situation where a man thinks he has a financial problem. Looking closely we see that, like Doug, he has lost jobs over and over because he gets angry with his bosses. When he leaves one job, he chants for another and then loses that one.

If he thinks his problem is his bosses, he is looking outside of himself for the cause of the problem. He may chant for another job and get it—the benefit. But as long as he is unwilling to look within and change his pattern of arrogance, which gives rise to his anger with his superiors, he will continue to lose jobs and his financial problems will continue.

Faced with a repetitive situation like this, he needs to chant to understand what it is in him that is the root of the problem. When he uses the practice in this manner, his desires can lead to self-knowledge and to awakening.

In awakening, the man would acquire wisdom, which would show him how to break through the behaviors which have led to problems in the past. In changing the behaviors, the man would be able to create a different outcome, becoming stable in his work life and also his financial life.

If you chant like this—to understand what you need to change inside yourself to modify your situation—you now enter a completely different and progressive path of life. These experiences will deepen your faith and lead to more confidence when faced with the next challenge.

Earthly desires then become the springboard through which you release yourself from the patterns, which are bringing you suffering.

We have seen the beginning of this process with Doug's attempts to modify his behavior at work. In his final talk with George, he came to understand that he had been holding onto his job by a string, until the last three weeks when he worked hard to change his behavior.

Maybe Doug will be able to grasp what George has shown him—that the changes in his attitude and behavior are leading to a positive work situation. If Doug persists with the practice, despite his disappointment, he will have started to walk the great path of inner transformation, which will ultimately lead to his happiness.

19

The Ninety-Day Experiment Continues

Nancy never did get around to calling Hanako the next day. Early the following evening, the phone rang. Nancy, who'd been hoping Doug would hear from one of the men, found herself listening to see who it was.

"Oh, hello Rob." Doug sounded depressed. "I lost my job." Reluctantly, Doug added, "Okay, I guess." He hung up and turned to her. "They're coming over again," he said glumly.

Nancy cheered inwardly. Doug could really use the support. He'd been sitting around moping all day. She couldn't imagine what he'd do on Monday when she left to work and he had nowhere to go. They started to pick up magazines and newspapers, and tidied the living room.

Rob and Scott, along with a short woman with a pixie haircut, walked in. Scott introduced her. "This is my wife Terri." Nancy was pleased to have a chance to meet another woman practitioner.

The five of them settled down in the living room. Right away Doug took charge.

Planting his feet firmly on the floor, chin jutting out, he said, "I don't see the point of all this. The chant doesn't work or I wouldn't have lost my job." Oh

178

dear, thought Nancy. *I hope he won't lose his temper.* She glanced at Terri to see how she was reacting.

Terri seemed relaxed and looked understanding. She nodded. "I can understand why you would feel discouraged."

Quietly, Rob said, "Tell me what happened."

Doug blurted out the whole story.

Scott, who had listened carefully, said, "Sometimes, something has to shift or an obstacle has to move before you can arrive at your goal. Can I tell you a story of my own?"

Terri nodded, her eyes sparkling, "This is a good story."

"I guess." Doug tipped his chair back and crossed his arms over his chest.

The sun was just setting and streaks of red-orange light flooded through the window and across the floor. Nancy hoped the story would calm Doug and help him see chanting in a more positive light.

Scott settled back comfortably, resting his arm on the back of the couch. "Twenty-five years ago when I was still early in the practice, I took a job which gave me the opportunity to train to succeed my boss's position. He was due to retire the next year. Working with him was difficult. He was very negative."

"Why didn't you just quit?" asked Doug.

"I had chanted for this kind of opportunity and it looked perfect. I just had to get through the time until he left."

"I think I'd have tried for something else."

"I thought about it, believe me, but I didn't want to lose this chance. Instead, I went to talk to one of my mentors in the practice. He advised me to chant for my boss's happiness."

"See what I mean?" Doug exclaimed. "This all seems crazy."

"I thought it was crazy advice too, but I'd asked for guidance so I decided to try it."

Doug looked suspicious. "So what happened?"

"Nothing, right away. About a month later, while I was chanting, I got the idea of transferring the company books onto the computer. The CFO gave me permission to go ahead. Not long after, I discovered my boss had been skimming money from the company for the last twenty years."

"Really?" Doug and Nancy blurted out together. Startled, they looked at each other and laughed.

Doug leaned forward intently, his disinterested air gone. "What did you do?"

Scott said, "I was horrified by the discovery, and now had a terrible dilemma. I ended up going over my boss's head to his superior, who called a Saturday morning meeting. My boss admitted everything."

Nancy could see that Doug was fascinated in spite of himself. "Did he get prosecuted?"

"That's what I was afraid of. I felt terrible. Since this whole situation had come to light due to me, I chanted even harder for my boss's happiness."

Nancy held her breath.

"The board met and decided not to prosecute but did ask him to leave and pay restitution. I was promoted into my boss's position."

"What a way to reach your goal!" Nancy said.

Scott shook his head as though he still couldn't believe it himself. "My feelings exactly. I felt badly about it for weeks. Then I happened to run into someone who knew my former boss well. I asked how he was doing. He told me that since his retirement my former boss had become very happy. Hearing that absolutely blew my socks off. He'd acted negatively toward me because of his guilt. After that experience, I knew the practice worked. I've chanted twice a day ever since."

Nancy couldn't contain herself. "So, you're saying anything can happen when you chant for a goal, but you can't predict how it's going to happen?"

All three practitioners nodded. "That's right," Rob said. "Anything can happen, so don't give up. It's important to handle your doubts. If you give in to them, you will never reach your goal."

Doug looked very thoughtful. He stretched out his legs and looked at the floor. "I just can't see that it's working."

Terri leaned forward. "I have to disagree. Haven't some things changed already?" She ticked off points on her fingers. "So far, you've modified how you handle things at work. Your boss recognized your efforts and is now willing to give you a recommendation. I'd say that's a lot for three weeks. If you hadn't been able to get that recommendation, where would you be?"

Boy, that's the truth, thought Nancy.

Terri smiled at Doug. "Looks to me as though your life is making a shift into a more positive direction. See what I mean?"

Doug rubbed his forehead, as if considering Terri's words. "I guess that's true," he admitted. "So what should I do now?"

Rob didn't hesitate. "Continue chanting then act to the best of your ability on ideas which come to you while you're chanting. Here are some things to read, which might help you hang in there." He handed Doug three articles. Nancy was very curious about them. She'd had some doubts of her own and could use a little encouragement. In spite of her dismay about their situation, she felt more hopeful than she had when they all walked in the door. *I hope they are right. Otherwise, what will we do?*

When the door closed behind Scott and Terri, Doug turned to Nancy. "I really don't know what to think about all of this," he said, raking his fingers through his hair. "It doesn't seem to be working for me, but they seem so sure about it."

Nancy looked him straight in the eye. "I've decided to give it the ninety days they've mentioned. I'm working on a goal of my own. In ninety days, I'll see where I am with it."

"What kind of goal?"

Nancy hesitated. She wasn't sure she wanted to tell him about her ambitions for work just yet. The timing was terrible, but she also wanted their relationship to be open and honest. She decided to go ahead. "I have some ideas to make the front office more welcoming to people. I've decided to take Scott's advice to be the best employee I can be and see if I can land a promotion."

"Well, I hope you have a better result than I've had." Nancy thought Doug looked a little more heartened than he had before they'd arrived.

She brushed her fingers through his hair. "Remember the twists and turns and what Rob said about giving in to doubt?"

182

"I know, I know." Doug grumbled but gave her hand a squeeze.

Nancy smiled at Doug. "I like the idea of considering this an experiment. That's how the new people's group told me to think of it. And, I have to say I'm very curious about how it's going to work out."

Doug nodded slowly. "If I could think of it as a ninety-day experiment and not have to believe in what I'm doing," he said, "maybe I could hang in there for ninety days."

Nancy's hopes jumped at Doug's change of attitude. "The group described it as a prove-it-to-yourself practice. At this point, no one expects you or me to have faith. How could we? I'm thinking of chanting more as an adventure myself."

Doug didn't reply. Nancy froze, wondering if she'd said too much. Then Doug spoke, sounding more positive than before. "If I don't have to believe in it, I'll give it another try. After these last three weeks, it'd be fun to have an adventure."

Nancy's heart leaped. From her own experience, she knew Doug's confidence would grow if he actually did chant on a regular basis. "I'm glad," she said. "An adventure together." They smiled at each other.

To The Reader

Handling Doubts

When you live in the world of illusion, one of the hardest things to believe is that every day you create your life and that you have full responsibility for what happens to you. It's equally hard to believe that you have a Buddha nature, which allows you to create life as you wish it. In fact, some people find these ideas frightening. They don't want that much responsibility. Most practitioners regard these concepts as liberating, as they have the power to change anything in their lives they don't like. But each person has to prove it to him or herself.

When faced with obstacles or adversity in any form, it's easy to doubt your true nature and disbelieve that you have the power to change your circumstances. No doubt you've faced a similar experience in your own life. But when doubts arise, remember that everyone is faced with difficulties at one time or another. Everyone has doubts.

If you're new to the practice, it's important that you ask questions to resolve your doubts. If you let these doubts take over, you won't be able to overcome the obstacle you are facing. Unless you deal with doubt, you will never know through experience that you are a Buddha, that you possess this great power within.

Doug is entirely new to the practice. He is discouraged and naturally is besieged by doubts. He's facing a big obstacle in his life, not only a big obstacle, but one which has become a pattern in his life. So how can he handle his doubts and step by step begin to build his faith?

First, he could take his doubts to a long term practitioner with years of experience. That practitioner will have learned how to handle doubts. He or she will have proved the practice over and over to himself. He will be able to give Doug confidence from his own experience. As a new practitioner, you will probably need to borrow the faith of the more experienced practitioners until you have proven to yourself that, by using the practice, you can overcome any problem in your life.

You might be given this statement to read from Nichiren Daishonin's writings.

> "If you do not question and resolve your doubts, you cannot dispel the dark clouds of illusion, any more than you could travel a thousand miles without legs."

Writings of Nichiren Daishonin, p. 1031

The more experienced practitioner would then encourage Doug or you, if it were your question, to make a conscious effort to chant with a sense of trust in the Gohonzon and then to exert one hundred percent effort in dealing with the steps of the challenge. Repeatedly praying, then taking action, allows you to be successful in addressing each small issue day by day. You cultivate self-assurance and self-confidence as you take steps toward your goal.

New practitioners are encouraged to study some of the writings of Nichiren Daishonin, such as the quotation below. His writings can teach you about the promises and give you hope, and maybe more confidence that you can handle this situation.

"There can be no doubt about the sutra passages that say, 'This sutra can fulfill their desires, as a clear cool pond can satisfy all those who are thirsty'. And 'They will enjoy peace and security in their present existence and good circumstances in future existences."

Writings of Nichiren Daishonin, p. 412

You may also experience a setback that blindsides you in a crucial moment. Be aware that when you are closing in on your goal, you're most susceptible to giving into doubt.

"What we do, how we act at the crucial moment is what determines ultimate victory or defeat."

Daisaku Ikeda, World Tribune 5/18/2001, p. 11.

If you suffer a setback like this, you must not allow doubt to take over. Renew your determination so that you can win over your circumstances. If you give up at this point, and allow doubt to win, you will not reach your goal.

Long time practitioners have repeatedly experienced they are never deadlocked when they chant about an issue. After many such experiences, when they don't know what to do, they go to the *Gohonzon* for renewal and to break through the barrier. They also know:

"When we plant the seeds of self-doubt, only noxious weeds sprout. When we limit ourselves with low expectations, the growth of the tree of happiness immediately ceases. The power of growth, of improvement, the power to overcome all stagnation can break through every obstacle and transform a barren wasteland into a verdant field— that unstoppable power of hope resides right there in your own heart. It will well up from the rich earth of your innermost being when you face the future

without doubt or fear: 'I can do more, I can grow, I can become a bigger and better human being'—life and faith are a never-ending struggle to grow."

Daisaku Ikeda, Buddhism Day by Day, p. 66

As you continue to chant and exert one hundred percent effort, you'll gradually learn to trust that chanting works. The time will come when you'll have broken through and won over one obstacle after another. Then you'll know through actual proof that you do have the capacity not to be deadlocked by any circumstance. At that point, your self-confidence will become unshakeable and doubt will become a stranger to your life. For now, just chant and take action to the best of your ability to resolve your situation.

20

A Crisis and Growth

Nancy awoke and looked at the clock, midnight. What had awakened her? Her awareness drifted sleepily through her body. Nothing. But there had been something. Then, a slow tightening began around her abdomen, tighter, tighter, tighter and slowly relaxed. Half awake, she contemplated the sensation. It didn't hurt but what was it?

Adrenalin flooded her. She felt tense, frightened. Slow, intermittent tightening was how her labor had begun the last time. Oh no. She couldn't lose the baby. She'd been afraid she wouldn't be able to have any more children after placing the first one for adoption. She felt she didn't deserve to have another child. Sadness, loss, long familiar feelings visited her again.

Afraid, alone, and only fifteen years old, she'd waited too long to end the pregnancy. Her parents had supported her; she knew they loved her. Nancy even understood that she was too young to be a mother. But she'd still been devastated that her parents hadn't wanted to raise her daughter themselves and insisted she place the baby for adoption.

After the birth, Nancy had held her baby and named her daughter Betty. The next day, she'd released the child to the social worker. Nancy thought she'd die of grief. She'd never forget that wonderful milky smell. She'd cried for months.

Maybe if I just lie quietly, the contractions will stop. She glanced at Doug. He slept as if dead to the world, and turned over and burrowed more deeply under the covers. She hated to wake him. How would she explain why she hadn't told him she was pregnant? She wouldn't be able to go to work tomorrow though. Nancy sighed inwardly. She had to tell him.

She looked at the clock again. Five minutes since the last contraction. She tried to relax. Her heartbeat sped up. Her body didn't lie. It knew she was frightened.

Feeling wetness, she ran into the bathroom, flipping the switch. A red spot on her nightgown! She froze. If she didn't wake Doug now and get to the emergency room she might lose this baby. Was it already too late? She knew she should chant but there was no time. She willed herself to hold this baby. She couldn't go through losing another child.

She shook Doug. He mumbled something and turned over. She turned on the light and shook him again, hard. "Wake up, Doug."

His eyes opened. "What the?" He shielded his eyes. "Why is the light on?"

"Get up. I need to go to the hospital."

Doug looked utterly confused. "Why?"

"I'm having a miscarriage."

"A what?" He sat bolt upright. "A miscarriage? You're pregnant?"

Nancy just nodded through her tears.

Doug scrambled out of bed. He grabbed his pants. "How long have you known?"

Nancy hesitated. "Let's talk later. Get me to the hospital."

They dressed swiftly.

Doug said over his shoulder, "I'll start the car."

Nancy hurried. They'd deal with the emergency now. Later, they'd have to talk.

The fluorescent lights of the waiting room seemed cold when they raced in. Doug strode right to the front desk. "My girlfriend may be miscarrying."

The clerk motioned to a nurse.

She came over to Nancy. "Come with me," she said, taking her by the arm. "We're going to find you a bed where you can lie down. Are you bleeding?" Nancy nodded. A lump clogged her throat at the nurse's kind tone.

When Nancy settled onto the pillow, she suddenly started to shiver. She could hear her teeth chatter.

Right away the nurse saw what was happening and patted her shoulder. "You're shivering, I'll get you a heated blanket," she said, whirling on her heel, her rubber soles softly squeaking as she walked out the door.

After the nurse left the room, tears slipped down Nancy cheeks. She cupped her hands protectively over her abdomen and rocked gently. She knew she should chant but she was too upset.

Doug peeked in the room. "I called your sister. She'll be here shortly."

Nancy smiled weakly. "Thanks." Anxiety spiked. *Oh no! What if she says something about the first baby? I've never told Doug anything about it, but she doesn't know that.*

190

Dr. Barker, thankfully a woman doctor, arrived soon and examined her. "We're going to have to wait and see. You'll need to have bed rest for the next few days." Oh dear thought Nancy. How much sick leave did she have at work?

"I'm going to see about a light sedative so you can relax and sleep. I'll look in on you later." White coat flying, she left the room.

At that moment, her sister Sara poked her face around the door. "I'm so glad to see you," cried Nancy. Love and relief welled up. Even through her worry, she felt more protected and secure having her sister there.

Sara rushed in and gave Nancy a hug. "How are you, honey? Is the baby all right?"

"We don't know," said Doug. "This is a wait and see situation."

"Not like before," murmured Sara.

Nancy flicked a glance at Doug and saw he hadn't heard. She gestured at Sara willing her to understand, not to say anything else. She couldn't tell whether Sara had registered what she was trying to say to her.

The nurse returned. "Here's the sedative the doctor ordered." She gave Nancy a pill and a glass of water. "Now a little history." She positioned a clipboard with a form attached. "Is this your first pregnancy?"

Nancy gulped, hesitated. She gave Sara a panicked glance. Sara understood and moved to intervene. "Doug, will you come with me to get a cup of coffee?"

Then, as though in slow motion, Doug looked at the nurse puzzled and then his eyes narrowed and focused on her. "You've had another baby?" He sounded incredulous.

Nancy couldn't say anything. She was paralyzed. Doug looked as though someone had hit him. She closed her eyes. She didn't want to see the shock written clear on his face.

Finally she pulled herself together, her voice husky. "It was a long time ago. I was only fifteen, long before I met you."

Sara stood watching them. "I think I'll leave you to talk," she said and walked rapidly out of the room. The nurse remained, her eyes moving back and forth between them.

Doug sat on the side of the bed and took her hand. "I can't believe you didn't tell me. Why?"

"I'm so sorry. I didn't expect you to find out like this. I've just tried to put the whole sorry experience behind me."

"What happened to the baby?"

"She was placed for adoption. I've been so afraid that I wouldn't ever be able to have another baby and now I might miscarry, and I'm getting close to being too old to have children." Misery enveloped her. She burst out sobbing.

Doug took her in his arms and rocked her. "Now, now, don't cry. It's going to be all right. How long have you known?"

"A couple of months."

"And you didn't tell me?"

Nancy debated. Should she tell him how she really felt? Having his arms around her felt so good, so safe. But it hadn't been this way recently. She'd been frightened of him and his temper, particularly when he was drinking. She took a deep breath.

"We've been fighting a lot and it's crossed my mind that this relationship might not last. I just wasn't sure I wanted to tell you about the baby."

"When did you think you would get around to it?"

"I wanted to see how we were getting along, before I made a final decision."

"What final decision?" Doug looked apprehensive.

Nancy took another deep breath, twisting her hands, and blurted it out. "I'm not sure I'm going to stay with you. I'm afraid of your drinking and your temper and I've been afraid that the baby might not be safe with you."

Doug jerked away. "You've been thinking about leaving?"

Nancy nodded, eyes cast down.

His breath whooshed out. He held her shoulders and looked directly in her eyes. "You can't leave me. I want to marry you."

"If you do, some things are going to have to change. We can't go on as we've been." There, she'd said it. She felt both scared and relieved. She'd wanted to say that for so long. No matter what happened now, it was out.

Doug's jealousy reared its ugly head. "Is there someone else?"

"No, nothing like that," Nancy reached for a tissue and wiped her nose. She was exhausted. Then she felt the tightening again. Her heart sank. Not again.

Doug looked at her as though she was a complete stranger. "This is just too much. I need some air." He rushed for the door. Nancy wasn't sure but thought she might have seen a tear on his cheek as he turned his head away.

The nurse came over to the bed.

"I've had another contraction," Nancy said.

The nurse nodded. "I'll let the doctor know."

Left by herself, Nancy was rocked with a cascade of emotions. Sadness, loss, relief, glad she had finally said what was on her mind, and uncertainty about the future. As she started to relax, she realized she wouldn't have had the courage to tell Doug how she felt before she started chanting. She hoped she'd done the right thing, even though they had gotten along better for the last couple of days. The possible miscarriage had completely blindsided her. She curled up, crying. Soon the sedative took effect. She fell asleep.

To the Reader

Chanting To Change Your Karma

Nancy has just taken a big step forward in breaking through the karmic issues which have prevented her from living a full life in her relationship. Remember, karma is the causes set by your thoughts, words and actions in the past which are coming to manifest in the present.

Nancy has assumed a subservient role in relationships with men due to her family training. Letting them take the lead gave her a feeling of security, but underneath she really wanted to have a more equal partnership. She has allowed Doug to treat her without respect, as though her needs are not important. We have seen that, through the chanting, she has begun to recognize this pattern and has started to develop more confidence.

She has taken baby steps. First, she continued to chant despite Doug's objections. Second, she refused to go home from the district meeting, even though Doug wanted her to come with him. For the first time, she's taken charge of her own life and started to forge her own identity.

In this scene, she has set a firm boundary with Doug. "We cannot continue on as we are. Things are going to have to change." Assuming she holds to this and Doug does want to marry her and be a part of raising their child, he will have to make changes of his own.

If you've ever begun to shift the way you behave, other people close to you might have worried. Changing, or rocking the boat, doesn't feel comfortable. The relationship feels unfamiliar and others in your life are likely to try to make you go back to behaving the way you did before. Habitual ways of relating to another person do not change without resistance. Changes, if they occur, will not be predictable or comfortable for Doug or Nancy.

When you start to chant Nam-myoho-renge-kyo your life can come to resemble a gardener first turning on an unused hose in the spring. Often, the first water that comes out is muddy and dirty. It is only when the water continues to run that it will turn clear. Like that, when you first start to chant, the water of your life might initially be muddy. There will be issues to resolve, which are keeping you from being happy. But, if you continue to chant, the kinks in your life will straighten out and your life will become progressive. You will be able to walk the pathway to happiness.

> "Although various karmic offenses and impediments may collect in our lives like frost or dew, Nichiren teaches we can eliminate their negative influences through the sun of Nam-myoho-renge-kyo. As we strive in our faith and practice based on the Gohonzon, we can cause the sun of our innate Buddhahood to rise from the depths of our lives, thus wiping out all our negative karma.
>
> This illustrates the Nichiren Buddhist concept of changing negative karma at life's innermost core.

SGI Study Department, The Essentials of Nichiren Buddhism (35) Changing Karma, reprinted in Living Buddhism May-June '06 p. 71, 72

21

Lessons, Lessons, Lessons

Doug raced down the hospital steps, tears in his eyes. Nancy was pregnant! How could she be thinking of leaving! He might be a father in just a few months! He'd just lost his job! How could he support a child?

He burst through the doors to the outside walking rapidly, his footsteps echoing on the quiet street. A church bell started to strike. One a.m. He was sure there was a bar a couple of streets over where he could get a drink.

The Starlight Lounge had one stool open at the bar. So much for a comfortable booth, he thought. Chatter filled the room. He settled on the stool and ordered a martini. The first swallow slid smoothly down his throat, leaving a trail of warmth which spread out in his stomach. He ordered another. His anxiety lessened.

Later, a little tipsy, he left his place to go to the bathroom. Upon his return, he saw that a big man, dressed in a conservative grey suit with a black and red tie, had taken his stool.

Doug's temper ignited. The nerve of that guy! Doug pointed to his jacket. "Hey, Mac. You're sitting on my frigging jacket. Move it."

The man gave him a bleary look and leaned back against the bar. "Buzz off," he growled.

Doug felt his rage mount. The loss of his job, the whole demoralizing evening rushed to the fore. He focused on the creep in front of him and he smashed the drunk in the face. The man rocked back then planted himself more firmly on the stool. He leaned back on the bar, mayhem evident in his glare. A man on the other side of him stood up.

Doug hesitated one second, then grabbed the interloper and pulled him off the stool. The second man stepped forward and punched Doug in the stomach and then on the side of the head. He lost his breath and saw stars. The drunk abruptly let go of him. Doug sprawled on the floor. He struggled for breath. The bartender yelled, "Break it up, all of you. I'm calling the cops."

Doug climbed heavily to his feet, feeling shaky. He leaned on the bar, while he tried to clear his head. The bartender looked straight at him and said, "You need to get a handle on that temper buddy. It's going to get you into a lot of trouble." A contemptuous look. "Get out. Now." The two men chuckled at his predicament.

Doug grabbed his coat and beat it out of the bar. Rage still boiled. He raced to his Camaro and peeled out. He whipped around the empty streets and headed for the expressway. Just as he raced over an expressway bridge, he spied a cop sitting in the dark. His heart dropped. "Nuts," he muttered. "He saw me."

Doug glanced at the speedometer. He was going ninety. Adrenalin raced through him. He couldn't be picked up, not half drunk. The cruiser's red lights flashed behind him. He slowed the car, finally coming to a stop. The police officer climbed out of his cruiser.

Doug fumbled for his license. The words tumbled out, pressured. "I know I was going fast. My girlfriend is in the hospital and I wanted to get back."

"Going this fast could have gotten you there on a stretcher. Step out of the vehicle." His voice was firm.

Doug opened the door. A rush of adrenalin flooded his chest. The officer was trying to see if he was drunk! A DUI would create real problems with Nancy.

The officer put Doug through his paces. Using all his powers of concentration, Doug managed to keep his balance.

The officer sighed. "All right. I'm just going to give you a ticket for speeding." The officer ran the light over Doug's cheek. "Looks as though you've been in a fight." Doug put his hand up to his cheek to hide the bruise.

"It's nothing important. I'm all right." He looked up. Other drivers were watching him as they drove by. He flushed.

The officer handed Doug a ticket. "Slow down now and get to the hospital in one piece."

Doug stared at the ticket. Three hundred fifty dollars! He groaned inwardly. This was all they needed right now, without his salary coming in. That, plus the fight didn't make this the best night of his life. He started slowly. The cruiser followed him for about a mile, while Doug's heart pounded, and then abruptly swung across the highway and headed back the direction it had come. He sighed in relief.

If he kept on like this, Nancy might decide she didn't want to stay with him. Then what? He hadn't just lost his job, he might lose her too. Then what about the baby? Everything he'd worked to build in his life was disappearing in front of him. He had to make sure that didn't happen. As unnerved as he was at the idea of being a father, he didn't want to be cut out of this child's life.

Even though they hadn't been getting along so well, he still wanted Nancy. She hadn't felt close enough to him to tell him about her first pregnancy. His heart sank. He felt a lump in his throat and then anger. Why? He shook his head and drove home. He needed to clean up before going back to the hospital.

To the Reader

Tumbling the Taro

In the Philippines, there is a potato-like tuber called the taro. The tuber is covered with a coarse black skin. In order to remove the skin, taros are placed in a basin of running water and tumbled together. The rubbing of one taro against another allows the skin to come off and the delicious tuber to appear.

Relationships between two people often serve the function of "tumbling the taro." When you find yourself in conflict with another person, you have the opportunity to see your hard bumps, or places where you need to change.

In his relationship with Nancy, Doug is facing a similar turning point where his own hard bumps are visible. He can continue living as he has been, perpetuating destructive elements such as his problems with alcohol and anger. Or, he can decide to do something different and change the way he's been living.

Remember the Buddhist principle discussed in chapter ten, called "oneness of self and environment?"

> *"Rather than there being one static environment that we living beings are all born into, every environment is uniquely customized, tailored to suit each of us according to the state of our inner lives. They are the causes and conditions into which we were born and reflect the effect of our past causes.*

*It begins with the parents to whom we were born
and extends through time and space to include all
the circumstances of our lives."*
Bill Aiken,   *World Tribune* 11/21/03, 7

Applying this principle, a practitioner knows that whatever is happening in his or her life has come from the inside
out. This is true, even though the situation appears to be
the fault of someone else. A practitioner, using the practice, would chant to understand his contribution to the
situation in order to be able to resolve it.

*"If we understand that the Ten Worlds manifest
themselves in the environment in a way that can be
deeply influenced by our own lives, then our path
becomes clear. To better influence our outer world,
we strengthen and improve the inner self."*
Bill Aiken, *World Tribune* 11/21/03, 7

This does not mean that the whole relationship situation is your fault. It does mean that you are involved to
some degree and, when one person changes, the other
person has to change as well. It could work equally well
with your partner making the changes, but we can only
change ourselves.

At this point, Doug isn't really using the practice. He
may continue in his habitual way, refusing to take responsibility for his actions and blaming his problems on someone else. But if he refuses to look at his situation and continues as he has been doing, his life will continue to move
in its current downward trajectory.

If you are dealing with a relationship issue, this would
be a good time to try using the practice to resolve it. It
is difficult to recognize and accept the fact that even
though the problem seems to be someone else's, you
have attracted the situation into your life and can change
it. Knowing and acting on this profound principle allows

each person to modify karmic patterns that may have existed for many, many years.

You may ask how you could approach such a situation. For example, you could chant to understand the problem and what you need to do. Or, you could chant for its resolution and then act on any ideas you may receive regarding steps you can take to resolve it. It's always good to talk to more experienced practitioners for support, especially when you feel blocked.

Nancy is using the practice to change herself. She has faced her fear of asserting herself, and has begun to take care of herself in the relationship. She is now chanting at home, whether or not Doug approves, and has finally told him he cannot continue the behaviors which are hurtful to her or she will leave him.

She has taken a first step at work. She changed her image from a person who couldn't handle her life to a competent person, and she is now contemplating taking steps at work to put her and her child on a more secure financial footing.

Note that Nancy chants to alter *her* life. She doesn't chant that others, including Doug, will modify their behavior according to her liking. The "tumbling of the taro" concept applies to places in her life which need to change.

We are seeing that she is revealing the delicious tuber within, through using relationship issues to transform old and non-productive ways of behaving. You can do this as well, bringing your beautiful inner nature to the fore.

You too can walk the path which will lead to your future happiness.

⚓ 22 ⚓

Chanting Leads to Action

At five a.m. the next morning, a red-headed nurse awakened Nancy and took her blood pressure and temperature. For a moment, Nancy was disorientated. Then she remembered she was in the hospital.

"Have you had any more contractions?" The nurse's eyes were friendly and Nancy warmed to her.

"No, everything seemed to settle down after I took the medication."

The nurse smiled. "Good. The doctor wants you to have bed rest for a couple of days. She wants you to relax and not worry about anything."

"Oh no," groaned Nancy. She'd have to take time off work. If she had to stay in the hospital for any length of time, she and Doug might not have any income at all.

After the nurse left the room, Nancy chanted quietly. She felt a little odd chanting in the hospital, but she couldn't ignore issues that needed work. She'd had enough experience with the practice to know she'd have more courage and deeper understanding of the issues if she chanted about them. As she repeated Nam-myo-renge-kyo she felt the shift that altered her state of consciousness. She felt connected to something bigger than she was.

To settle her concern about their finances, she chanted for stability with their income.

She chanted for a healthy full term baby. She could feel her heart swell with delight as she put her hands protectively on her abdomen. She shifted her weight. The bed wasn't as comfortable as sitting on a chair at home.

She started the chant again, this time for clarity about her relationship with Doug.

She'd been so impressed at first. She didn't have a college degree and Doug held an MBA. But MBA or not, he was having difficulty holding onto jobs. She hadn't expected that.

He'd seemed so sophisticated, too. He'd taken her out to dinner and ordered wine like a connoisseur. But his drinking wasn't fun anymore. It was causing problems. She adjusted the pillows behind her back so she could sit straighter.

Then there was his possessiveness. She hadn't recognized it as a need to control. When they were dating, she'd felt protected. But, once they were living together, she felt suffocated. She needed to know if Doug could change the drinking or the possessiveness before making any decisions.

She heard footsteps on the linoleum in the hall and recognized Doug's walk. She chanted a final slow Nam-myoho-renge-kyo.

He carried a bouquet of red roses and the delicate blooms of white baby's breath. She exclaimed with pleasure. It was like it had been when they were first courting. He was always romantic then.

While he put them in a vase, she noticed the discoloration on his cheek. She looked more closely. The right side of his face looked bruised. "Is that a bruise on your cheek? What happened to you?"

Doug flushed and put his hand to his cheek. "I was pretty upset last night. I went to a bar a couple of blocks away to have a drink. A guy grabbed my place when I went to the restroom. He started a fight and I had to defend myself."

Nancy sighed. "Oh, Doug."

Doug looked away. "It was no big deal." In a low voice he said, "Are you really going to leave me?"

Nancy took a deep breath. All at once she was warring with herself—to tell him the truth, or make him feel better, as she usually did. She hated having to confront him. He would get angry and she wasn't sure she could handle that right now. On the other hand, if she didn't tell him the truth, nothing was going to change.

Scared but determined, she sat up straighter against the pillows and looked him directly in the eyes. "I'm very worried about your drinking and your temper. The drinking has gotten worse and, when you drink, you are an entirely different person."

Doug held up his hand. "Wait a second. I was upset. Why can't I have a drink when I'm upset?"

Nancy couldn't believe he didn't see the problem. "Look what happened! You ended up in a fight. You can't stay in control of your temper when you've been drinking."

Doug was dismissive. "You're making entirely too much of that fight. It was minor."

Nancy's voice rose. "You aren't listening to me. This is one of the problems. Is your drinking more important than our relationship?"

His eyes grew cold, his voice clipped. "Of course not." Then he shook his finger at her. "But I won't have a girl-friend who tries to control me."

Nancy's temper snapped. "But you can control *me*. Is that it? I can't go out unless you let me. I can't do things that interest me, because you aren't interested, or because you want me home all the time." She shouted, "That doesn't work for me. I'm important too."

Doug's eyes flashed. She knew he was warning her to back off, but she couldn't. Not now. The words poured out.

"I can't have a life of my own living with you. I feel smothered and I want a relationship where we can both do the things we want to do."

Doug shifted in his chair, planted his feet on the floor and leaned forward. He pointed a finger. "You've changed since you started that chanting."

Nancy paused. Was it the chanting? In a flash of in-sight she saw that she *had* changed. Without doubt it was due to the chanting. She was stronger, less willing to knuckle under. "Don't point your finger at me Doug. I'm finally telling you how I feel. Before, I didn't."

"Like you hid your first pregnancy from me?"

It was Nancy's turn to flush. Heat rose from her chest into her face. "I don't tell everyone about that. Frank-ly, I haven't been sure enough about our relation-ship." Then, unmistakably, she felt a slight contraction. The bleeding began again. Her heart plummeted. "Oh no!" she wailed. "It's started again."

Doug raced out of the room. Nancy looked out of the window, conscious only of her fear of losing the baby.

The nurse returned with him. "You're bleeding again?"

Nancy nodded miserably. She could feel the tears coming. "I'm so scared."

The nurse calmly said, "Many women have some bleeding and still carry the baby to term. You need as little stress as possible." She glanced back and forth from Doug to Nancy and said, "I heard you arguing. That isn't helping."

They both looked at one another.

Relieved, Nancy addressed Doug. "I guess we can't discuss this right now."

Doug hesitated. "Maybe not right now, but we have to talk about it soon."

"I know." Nancy closed her eyes and lay back against the pillow.

Doug walked out to find some breakfast. Nancy could see that he was upset. He walked a little hunched over, as though he had taken a body blow. Her heart went out to him. Underneath that bravado, he was insecure. She felt badly that she'd had to force him to look at his life, but he had to face what was happening if there was any chance for them to stay together.

Even after Doug left, Nancy's heart continued to pound. She was scared and exhilarated. She'd finally done it! She'd told him everything. She felt as though a big load had rolled off her back. But, she also felt apprehensive about next steps.

She curled up in the bed and reflected on what life would be like if they broke up. Nothing had been decided today, that was for sure. After that discussion she was afraid Doug was unwilling to change. It was too early to know though. She wished he'd chant, but he was so stubborn.

The baby seemed more real somehow. She felt over-whelmed. What if she had to work and raise a child, do it all by herself? Could she? Could she handle it physically? It certainly would be a lot easier if Doug were working. Then she could settle down. She warmed at the thought. She'd like to be able to stay home.

But if nothing had changed and he still wasn't working, it wouldn't be any easier for her. If she had to work, she didn't think she could leave the baby with him, not with that temper. She let out a slow breath. At least she didn't have to do anything today, thank goodness. She had some time.

Chanting quietly to herself, her worry receded. She felt protected and calmed. She let her body relax. Making sure she held onto the baby was her top priority now. She picked up the phone to let Annette know what was happening.

To The Reader

Learning about Human Revolution

As you can see in this chapter, Nancy's made real changes in the manner she's lived her life until now. When she started the practice she was shy and introverted, saying little of how she felt about anything. She tended to allow other people to control their relationships with her.

Once she practiced consistently, she became stronger. In this last discussion with Doug, she's altered her usual way of behaving. In the past, she wouldn't tell him what she thought in order to protect his feelings and to protect herself from his anger.

Instead, this time she addressed the elephant in the room, his abuse of alcohol. When he dismissed her she didn't back off but instead came out and told him what she really thought about how he behaves when he is drinking and how she can't tolerate his controlling ways.

Her guide, Hanako would say she has embarked upon the process of her human revolution.

Human revolution in Buddhism doesn't refer to a political event, but has quite a different meaning. This revolution doesn't occur outside the individual but rather within each person.

"Human revolution" is a term used by Josei Toda, the second president of the Soka Gakkai, to describe the process by which individuals gradually expand their lives, conquer negative and destructive tendencies, and ultimately make

212

the state of Buddhahood their dominant life-condition."

(www.sgi-usa.org)

In Buddhism, human revolution will result in you overcoming your weaknesses. Through practice you will become more and more your authentic self. This will lead you to satisfying work and place you on a path which will lead you to discover your unique purpose in life. You will come to manifest the person you have the potential to become.

Gradually, the way you've lived your life until now will give way to fundamental changes. In Nancy's case she's becoming stronger and less introverted. Now that she can express what she needs in a relationship, she will be more likely to find herself with more friends and living a life that is more satisfying. Many people who have based their lives on anger find that, when their anger disappears, they too can enjoy their lives more and have more satisfying relationships.

Daisaku Ikeda says that our struggle in our human revolution is to become as strong an individual as possible and to develop compassion and mercy. Human revolution is clearly seen in the life of an individual when a person broadly expands his or her state of mind. Hope, vitality, wisdom, compassion and good fortune will then well forth from within our lives.

Initially, this process might appear a little mysterious. You might ask, how does it happen? President Toda describes how this comes about in a comfortable and natural way.

"You don't have to worry about changing your personality. All you have to do is chant daimoku (Nam-myoho-renge-kyo) and live the best that you can. Then, very naturally, you will see the negative aspects of your personality disappear, leaving you with the positive ones. You must have a clear purpose and work for the betterment of society."
Josei Toda, *Faith Into Action*, p 131

As you work on your human revolution, chanting and doing *gongyo* twice a day and taking the actions to overcome challenges, you'll find yourself gradually becomeing stronger physically, intellectually, and spiritually.

It doesn't happen overnight but it will happen. You'll become aware of the limitless power inherent in your life and become able to draw it out and use it. Through this profound reformation in the depth of your life, true happiness develops. It is the roadmap to happiness, guaranteed.

⟪23⟫

Who Said It Would Be Easy?

Nancy walked into their living room, glad to be out of the hospital. The air felt stale. The flowers she'd put on the coffee table had been left to wilt. *Hadn't Doug noticed them at all?*

She opened the window and let in some fresh air. It smelled so good after the hospital's atmosphere of sickness. She took a deep breath, letting it wash away the faint queasiness, a daily reminder of the developing life inside her.

She noticed what looked like a traffic ticket on the table next to the recliner. Curious, she went over to examine it and saw he'd gotten it the night she'd gone into the hospital. *Three hundred fifty dollars! Good heavens. What had he done?* She looked for the offense on the ticket but then heard his heavy footsteps on the stairs and hastily put the ticket back on the table.

They hadn't pursued the relationship discussion since the day in the hospital. Without saying a word, both had let it go for the time being, until the danger of miscarriage passed. Nancy dreaded talking to Doug, but that discussion had to take place soon.

Now she was home and facing it, she wasn't sure she felt ready. She felt tense just thinking about it. She had to do it though.

She slipped into the second bedroom. Better chant for a few minutes to boost her confidence. She'd need her strength.

She settled into a comfortable chair. Good thing she didn't have to sit like a yogi. She'd be too stiff. She started to chant aloud quietly, feeling her body slowly relax. She was glad she didn't have to clear her mind. Hanako had told her just to set an intention. She shifted her leg. Her foot was trying to go to sleep.

She wanted to use this time to get a deeper perspective on her relationship with Doug. Sinking into the rhythm of the chant, she recalled their last conversation. She felt that shift in consciousness which she now recognized as signaling she was connected to something larger than herself.

All at once she experienced a profound realization. She couldn't change Doug. He had to do that himself. Relief swept over her. She didn't have to wait for him to change! She had already started to take charge of her own life, by not letting him control whether she chanted and by telling him how she felt. Strength and confidence welled up. Her back straightened.

Then she made up her mind. For the baby's safety, if he couldn't get a handle on his temper or his drinking, she couldn't stay with him. The only question was how long would she wait for him to change.

Interesting, she thought. She always understood issues more deeply after chanting about them.

She heard Doug pass by the door as he carried her bag to the bedroom and then went directly to the kitchen. She held her breath. Was he going to make a drink? Fear rose in her body as she waited to hear the ice cubes clink. Nothing happened. She shook herself mentally. *I don't have to be afraid. I can be strong no matter what he does.*

She ended her chanting with a final Nam-myoho-renge-kyo and went to join him in the living room. He carried a bag of chips but no drink. She settled back on the couch.

He dropped into his recliner, crunching chips. He offered her the bag. She shook her head. His hair was a little mussed. Different from his usual neatness. She suppressed a wish to smooth it. "Why are you staring at me like that?" he asked.

Nancy felt defensive, but set her feeling aside. She wasn't going to let him make her feel that way. She said, "We need to talk now."

He nodded with a glum look on his face, gazing at the floor. "There's something else I need to tell you. The night I got into the fight I got a speeding ticket."

Nancy remained calm. "I saw the ticket. I'm glad you told me." *Boy, his drinking was costing them.*

"Your salary won't cover it." Doug said.

Tiredness and anxiety swept over her. "I don't know what to do."

Doug nodded. "I'll have to figure out something, I guess."

That's what you always say, thought Nancy. "You'd been drinking, hadn't you, when you got the ticket?"

Doug shifted his weight. "Oh now, honey. Don't start that." He climbed out of the recliner and put an arm around her. "Sometimes I feel as though I don't know you anymore. You used to be easier to get along with, sweeter or something. I liked you better the way you were." He knelt down beside her and gave her a kiss. "Be the way you used to be, honey."

Nancy felt the temptation to give in and then a flash of guilt. *He was so handsome.* Mentally she pushed both the attraction and the guilt aside. She could hear her mother say that men don't like strong women. Women were the weaker sex, after all. Anger flashed through Nancy. Why in the dickens was weakness good? She didn't understand it. But she wasn't going to give up this sense of confidence to start living in a cage again. She took a deep breath and shrugged off his arm.

"You're right. I began to change after I started chanting on a regular basis. It's been good for me. I'm stronger."

Doug frowned. "It's not good for me! I need a relationship where . . ."

"Where *you* can be in charge?" Nancy forced herself to stay focused.

A red flush spread over his face. He nodded. "I guess so. That's the way it should be."

Nancy was surprised. *He'd actually admitted it.* She'd known he felt this way and had thought she could live with it. But the reality had been very different from what she had thought it would be. Tension swept over her. Relax, she thought. The nurse had said she wasn't supposed to be stressed.

She bit her lip. "I've always wanted a relationship, which could be more." She tried to find the right word. "Like a partnership." *There, she'd said it.*

Doug looked shocked, as though he'd never considered this. A pause. Then the words rushed out. "You aren't the way you used to be, when we got along so well. Be my girl again." His blue eyes searched hers. She could smell the sweetness of his breath.

She felt herself leaning into him. He could be so attractive when he wanted to be. Maybe they could be a family.

Her chanting goals rushed back at her. It wasn't only about her anymore. She had a baby to think about. Her issues with Doug hadn't changed. Raising her chin, she said, "I wish I could be. But I can't live with your drinking or your temper. When you drink, your temper goes out of control. I don't want to be afraid all the time. I just can't live that way anymore."

Doug's face turned darker red. "You're telling me to stop drinking?"

"You don't have to stop. But I don't want to live with it anymore."

"You're not serious. You'd leave me with the baby coming?"

Nancy nodded.

His warm eyes turned glacial. His face hardened. "You'd leave when I need you the most?" His voice rose. "How can you be so selfish? Could you *really* manage alone?" Doug's words were filled with disbelief.

She straightened her shoulders. "Yes. It's not what I want, but I'm prepared to do it."

He flinched and then scowled. "I don't even drink that much. I go to work, don't I? Besides, I don't ask you to give up things you enjoy."

"Yes, you do," Nancy said. *Could Doug really be so blind?*

Doug jumped to his feet and paced around the room. "You're making a big deal out of nothing." He shot Nancy a wounded look. "Why are you trying to destroy everything we've built?"

She reacted to Doug's abrupt movement, but then found her ground again. She refused to feel guilty. She shouldn't have to live with this. Suddenly she understood what she was hearing. Her heart sank. "You're telling me that drinking is more important than our relationship or the baby?"

"No!" Doug shouted. "You're blowing all this completely out of proportion." The veins on his neck bulged. "Why are you are always on my back? You think you're perfect, Miss holier-than-thou?"

Nancy felt off balance. Did she behave that way? She took a deep breath to ground herself again. "This isn't my problem: it's yours," she said firmly. "You need to make a decision." Without another word, Doug wrenched open the door and clattered down the stairs. The front door slammed. The silence was deafening.

Nancy shook inside. A lump rose in her throat. She swallowed, trying to force it down. She had hoped, once he knew she was pregnant, he'd choose her and the baby. Tears prickled behind her eyes. She blinked them back. She didn't want to cry. She'd had such high hopes. She didn't want it to end this way. Tears overflowed and trickled down her cheeks. She fumbled for a tissue. Her stomach churned. Maybe she should apologize, take it back. Maybe she was being unreasonable.

Then she felt that determination revive once more. Her jaw set. *No. Not this time. I'm not going to live like this anymore.*

She felt the tension, as though the weight of the world had just settled on her shoulders. She was going to be completely alone, just her and the baby. What a bleak future. Had she made a mistake? Was she strong enough to do it by herself?

To the Reader

Modifying Behavior

Nancy has made a difficult decision. There will be challenges and obstacles as she works to establish a life for herself where she can be happy.

You might ask, if human revolution is this hard, why would I want to do it? Then ask yourself, don't the great challenges we face and overcome make us strong?

Envision an airplane racing down the runway. The hardest part of the flight is lifting free against the pull of gravity. The wind rushing under its wings gives the plane lift. By pushing against it the plane can take off. By the time it reaches altitude, the plane flies easily through the air.

Human revolution is much like the flight of a plane. It is hardest at the beginning. But as the resistance of the wind gives the plane lift, the obstacles which present themselves strengthen you to handle anything life can throw at you. Consistency in using the practice, and persistence in taking action toward addressing the difficulty, will enable you to overcome any obstacle.

As you challenge your human revolution, you will enter the process of change. Let's look at how this worked with Nancy.

First, she chanted to understand the nature of the problem she faced with Doug. While chanting, she realized that she couldn't change him but could change herself. This meant she had to do some things differently. She started to take charge of her own life by chanting despite his disapproval, and later by telling him at the hospital how she felt about his behavior and the relationship.

As she faced Doug at home, Nancy felt her courage slip away. She told herself she didn't need to be afraid of the discussion. When she felt defensive—her habitual pattern—she reminded herself to put it aside. When he accused her, and she felt guilty, she pushed the guilt aside and confirmed the chanting had made her stronger. When he lost his temper, she flinched but then confirmed that she shouldn't have to live with this.

Nancy is transforming lifelong behavioral habits. She is accustomed to being wrong in the relationship. She is used to letting her partner dominate. A part of her still loves Doug, even though she can't live with his behavior. At first, she reacts as she has habitually, defensive, guilty, and flinching. But chanting has made her stronger. She is able to catch herself, put aside those habitual reactions, and assert her newfound strength. She refuses to give in to Doug's attempts to bring her into line.

We see Nancy grappling with the same battle we all have within ourselves, a struggle between positive and negative forces.

Human revolution occurs as we overcome our negative side and establish the positive side. There are common steps in the process of change but they don't always happen in sequence. The steps of change can move forward, backward and then forward again.

During step one, you'll see how you could have behaved differently *after* the fact. In step two, you'll see the need to behave differently *while* you behave in the old way, as we saw with Nancy. She was able to catch herself and shift how she responded in the moment.

Sometimes you can see the need to behave differently, but in the stress of the moment, can't translate that insight into new behavior.

During the final step, you'll see the need to behave differently *before* you fall into the old pattern and then consciously change the behavior.

> *"Life is a process of ongoing challenge. Those who lead lives of boundless challenge realize boundless growth. In a time of tumultuous change, what people need most is vitality to challenge their circumstances and the wisdom to open the treasure house of knowledge, to ceaselessly strive to create new value."*
>
> Daisaku Ikeda, *Faith Into Action,* p. 15

Life becomes easier and more enjoyable as you overcome one weakness after another, gradually assuming control and steering your life onto its true course. Even though problems are part of life, your capacity to deal with them will improve.

As President Ikeda notes, Eiji Yoshikawa (1892-1962), the renowned Japanese author of many epic historic novels, asserted:

> *"Great character is forged through hardships. Surviving a life of hardships and difficulties, or stormy ups and downs, is what produces a person of great depth and character. True happiness is also found in such an unshakable state of life."*
>
> *Faith Into Action,* p. 143

Grappling with and overcoming difficulties is also the path toward building your faith. As you use the practice and surmount one obstacle after another, you will come to understand that you have a secret weapon in life—that, with the practice, it is possible to handle anything which might come up.

"*Faith makes people strong. And people of genuine faith shine the most when they encounter great difficulties. Certainly it is better not to have obstacles. But from another standpoint, difficulties are benefits. By challenging and overcoming them, we can forge a character pure and immutable as gold.*"

Daisaku Ikeda, *Faith Into Action*, p. 142

Human revolution can be challenging, but aspects of it can also be easy. For example, some people with bad tempers begin to chant and then find that their anger problems disappear without a lot of effort. As each person's karma differs, so the process of human revolution is different for each person who practices. But as you address the changes needed to living a full life, the end result will always be the same. You will overcome obstacles in life and make happiness an everyday reality.

24

Fundamental Darkness

Blinded by his rage, Doug stomped down the steps. He burst out the front door almost bumping a woman on the sidewalk. Seeing her startled look, he swerved.

Nobody's going to tell me to stop drinking! Acid welled up into his throat. He swallowed to clear it. *Nancy's not going to tell me how to handle my life!* His feet pounded the pavement as though to emphasize his thoughts. He shoulder brushed a tall man as he dodged around a couple walking ahead of him.

He continued his headlong rush. He passed a teetering older man Hey, slow down buddy!" The man quavered. Doug pounded on.

If she leaves, where will I live? Without a job I will be homeless! Fear lanced through him, followed by anger. *How can she abandon me like this?*

He stumbled on an old maple tree root. He slowed his pace but his thoughts raced on.

How can she be so selfish? I'm not going anywhere. If she wants her freedom so bad, let her move out. That would fix her good.

Doug heard footsteps behind him. He startled when the tall man grabbed him by the shoulder. "Hey, did you hear me? You're being a menace on the sidewalk."

"Bug off," growled Doug. He tried to shake off the restraining arm. The tall man frowned and held Doug's arm even tighter. "Calm down, young man. Take some slow breaths."

Doug realized how he must look to the people casting glances at them as they went by. He slowed his breathing. "I'm sorry, I'm upset."

The man released his arm. "Take it easy, okay?" Doug nodded. The man turned away.

Why was everyone trying to control his life? His boss and Nancy and now a total stranger.

Doug walked on more slowly. His anxiety built up again. He felt short of breath. He needed a drink. He spied a liquor store about halfway down the next block. He made a beeline for it. He didn't want to go home. He didn't know if he even had a home.

Ten minutes later, with a bottle of whiskey hidden inside a paper bag, he settled on a park bench. The booze warmed his throat and stomach as he sat and took swigs of whiskey. His anger, anxiety and sadness dulled. Everything mellowed.

He watched the sun fall gently behind the trees. Shadows lengthened. Across the grass, children played on the swings and in the sandbox. A lump came into his throat. He could have a child this age in just a few years. She couldn't break up with him, with the baby coming! He guzzled his bottle.

Nancy is abandoning me. She is just thinking of herself, not of what I need. Tears came and he let them flow. As dusk turned into darkness, parents collected their children and left the park.

Doug felt entirely alone. He sat, numb. He felt dizzy and sick. When he stood up, he stumbled. He was too drunk to walk. He felt sick and sank down onto the ground. He'd only sit here a few moments, just until the nausea passed and his whirling head cleared. He closed his eyes.

When Doug awoke the sun was up. He wished he hadn't awakened at all. He was on the ground. Cold, hard, wet. He smelled terrible. Every part of his body hurt.

A couple of school age boys were standing a little ways away, pointing at him and whispering. They ran to a young woman and pointed him out to her. He could hear her say to the boys, "Stay away from him. That man's a wino."

Wino! is that how I look? His mind felt fuzzy. He couldn't remember how he had gotten here or what had happened. He'd drunk a lot. Much too much. He lay quietly for a moment, trying to orient himself. Then he remembered with a jolt. Nancy was leaving. Because of his drinking.

This was all he needed, being found like a passed out drunk on the ground. He must look like a bum. He felt a day's growth of beard on his face. He flushed with embarrassment.

He felt his pocket. *Where is my wallet?* He ran his hand through both pockets, searching. Panic flooded him. He had his keys but not his wallet. His credit cards, his driver's license, the last of his money. He'd been rolled. Even his bottle was gone. He groaned. *What will I do without credit cards or ID?*

His head throbbed. His mouth was dry. He slowly climbed to his feet, stumbled over to a drinking fountain and splashed water over his face. His stomach growled but he couldn't handle the thought of food.

He looked up. Wasn't that Rob from the Buddhist group walking down the sidewalk? Doug remembered his kindness. Then Rob glanced in his direction but he didn't seem to see him. Doug quickly looked away, hoping Rob hadn't recognized him. Did he really look like a worthless drunk?

Last night, he'd gone out of control. It scared him. He'd lost everything, his job, his home, Nancy, the baby.

He trudged toward the apartment, avoiding the eyes of other people on the sidewalk. His thoughts clamored. His head pounded. Life couldn't get worse. Or could it? He didn't want to be one of those drunks that slept in doorways, homeless. He shuddered.

But, he didn't want to give up drinking either.

He contemplated his position. He was right on the verge of being homeless, one of those guys who pushed their possessions around in a cart and slept under a bridge. He could barely face the thought of rehab.

He reached the apartment and prayed that Nancy was at work. She couldn't see him the way he was right now. He'd clean up. He didn't think he needed rehab. That seemed a little extreme. He could do it by himself. If he proved to Nancy that his drinking wasn't a problem, maybe he could get her back.

To the Reader

Discovering That Life is a Mirror

Doug has gradually changed from a well-meaning, capable, but self-doubting person to someone who has lost control with alcohol. As he has allowed his hunger for alcohol to take over his life, he stopped recognizing that he is creating his own problems. We have seen his anger, his self pity, his disregard for others and his refusal to accept responsibility.

Remember the discussion about the ten worlds? The four lowest are:

Hell–(misery, feeling trapped and hopeless)

Hunger–(insatiable greed)

Animality–(where instinctual desires are followed without thought of the outcome, exploitation of others)

Anger–(rage and selfishness)

Doug has come to live more and more in these four lower worlds, as he has allowed fundamental darkness to take control of his life. At this point, he is living in Hell and not seeing a way out.

These four paths are called the four "evil paths" for good reason. If anyone allows them to grow unchecked in his or her life, each of these paths will ultimately lead to suffering.

Look at Doug's situation. He believes he is fully hemmed in by the actions of other people. His boss fired him. Nancy has thrown him out. He believes he has no place to go. So, he drinks to numb his fear and the pain of his situation.

On the surface, it would appear that he has reason to think this; he has no job, so how is he going to live? He doesn't see that his own actions have brought him to this and that he must make the changes to climb out of this hole. Instead he blames his boss, Nancy, and the man on the sidewalk for trying to control his life.

Doug doesn't realize they are mirroring back to him the fundamental darkness in his life. His boss pointed out that Doug's anger threatened his job. Nancy is showing him his selfishness, his inability to consider the needs of another person and the issues with his drinking. The man on the sidewalk has shown him his disregard for others and that his anger has gone out of control. He must address these issues in his life in order to become happy.

He continues to remain unaware of the fact that he has, within himself, a great jewel—a Buddha nature. When activated, it will show him the way out of any difficulty and allow him to overcome any obstacle. This ignorance, the disbelief and doubt regarding our essential nature, is the foundation stone of all fundamental darkness. This ignorance is why we sometimes let our problems overwhelm us. When overwhelmed, we don't believe that we have the capacity to overcome anything life throws at us.

Doug is not alone. Each of us has the dilemma and challenge to engage on a daily basis with the negative forces in our own lives—to overcome them and thereby become truly happy. Doug's been frightened by his experience in the park. But he has not yet made the decision to engage with the negative forces in his life.

If you have encountered the chant, the struggle with your own negativity can become easier. You have a tool which will enable you to turn any problem around into something positive for your life, to turn poison into medicine.

> "Daimoku, (Nam-myoho-renge-kyo) is like fire. When you burn the firewood of earthly desires, then the fire of happiness—that is, of enlightenment— burns brightly. Sufferings thus become the raw material for constructing happiness. For someone who does not have faith in the Mystic Law, sufferings may be only sufferings. But for a person with strong faith, sufferings function to enable him or her to become happier still."
>
> Daisaku Ikeda, *Faith into Action*, p. 143

25

See the Truth of the Matter

After Doug slammed out of the apartment, Nancy had trouble sleeping. She raised herself on her elbow to look at the clock for the umpteenth time. It was three a.m. and he still wasn't home.

All the old doubts surfaced. Did she have the right to push Doug to deal with his drinking? Her mother wouldn't have behaved that way, but would have accepted him as he was. But then she had something her mother didn't have, the chant.

Her first responsibility was toward this baby. Maybe being a single mother wouldn't be the best for the child, but living with Doug's problem couldn't be good either.

She twisted and turned, the sheets tangling around her legs.

She could still hear him shout that she was being selfish. She'd thought she was taking care of the baby and herself for the first time, but she still felt guilty. She'd been taught that it was selfish to put yourself first, you should always think of the other person.

She wouldn't be able to do anything tomorrow if she didn't get some sleep! Her pillow wadded up under her cheek.

In desperation, she decided to try chanting in bed, to see if she could relax. She curled up and began the chant. As the chant became rhythmic, her body relaxed. Sleep crept over her. Her last thought was that she'd sort it all out in the morning.

Light streamed into the bedroom window. Nancy could barely open her eyes. She realized, thankfully, she had one more day off before she had to return to work. Abruptly, she awakened fully. The other side of the bed was empty. Her solar plexus tightened. She was sure Doug had gone drinking and was worried that he might have had an accident. He'd never stayed out all night before.

While she busied herself scrambling some eggs and buttering her toast, she found herself rehashing all their issues. Her mind raced. She picked at her food. She tried his cell. No answer.

Firmly, she took herself in hand. "You're going in circles," she said aloud. "Go and chant about it." Finishing her breakfast, she walked to the living room and found her focal point. She settled onto the couch.

As she started to chant, her mind and body relaxed and focused. She reflected that it almost seemed as though she had entered into another reality, one with broader scope, vision and wisdom, as though she had a way of looking at the relationship from above rather than being stuck in the issues.

She reflected on the relationship, the chant rhythmically underlying her thoughts. Her early hopes for the relationship had not materialized. Now she was living with a man who was having trouble holding jobs, who was drinking more and more to bolster himself. As he did, his temper got worse. Over the last year he'd been walking a downhill path. Her own life had become more difficult as these changes had occurred in Doug. She knew he was struggling and she felt badly for him, but now she had to think about the baby. She rubbed her beads, stretched her legs and curled them under the chair.

The Ten Worlds came to mind. He was living more and more in the lowest four—Anger, Animality, Hunger, and the very lowest, Hell. If she stayed with him, she and the baby would be living in those worlds as well. She wanted much more than that. She wanted a life for her child in a happy family, living a life that was progressive and forward moving. She had to make a choice.

She just concluded chanting when she heard Doug's footsteps on the stairs and his key in the lock. As he opened the door, she heard him mutter, "Oh no, she's home."

Facing her stood a Doug she'd never seen before. He was unshaven and his hair was uncombed, messy, matted and dirty. She sniffed the air, liquor. His eyes were bleary and bloodshot. He must have a massive hangover.

"What happened? Where have you been?" she exclaimed. "You look like a drunk from the mission!" This Doug didn't look at all like the handsome, polished man she'd moved in with two years ago.

He flushed and looked away. "It's your fault. You upset me yesterday!"

The truth hit her with blazing clarity. He wasn't ready to change and she couldn't do it for him. Was this person she wanted to help her raise the baby? Her next step came crystal clear.

"That does it, Doug. You have a big problem with alcohol and I can't live with it. I want you to move out." She felt grounded, sure that she was doing the right thing. It felt so good to be finally taking care of herself and not waiting for Doug to change.

His face twisted. "Don't think you're going to throw me out. You're the one deciding to leave." He advanced toward her, raising his hand.

She stood up. "Don't you dare hit me. Think about the baby."

He dropped his hand, growling. "Don't start again Nancy. I can handle myself."

"No, you can't. Look at yourself." She wrinkled her nose. "For heaven's sake, go take a shower."

His face hardened but he turned and headed toward the bathroom, pulling his shirt over his head. Nancy ran to their bedroom and pulled out her largest suitcase. She started to throw clothes into it. Where could she go? She could go to Sara's or to her parents or to a hotel. No, not a hotel. That implied she'd be coming back. She wasn't coming back.

She knew what her parents would say. They hadn't wanted her to move in with Doug to begin with. And now she was pregnant. She sighed. They were going to find out soon anyway. But for now, maybe Sara was a better choice.

Moving swiftly, she tore her clothes off their hangers, and tossed them in the suitcase. Fortunately, she didn't have a lot of stuff to pack. She didn't know what she would do about the couch. They'd both paid for it. She looked around the room with finality. Her refuge didn't exist any longer. The couch was just furniture. She could leave it.

She heard the shower start. Maybe she could be gone before he finished showering. She guessed she'd leave her toothbrush and hairbrush in the bathroom. She didn't want him to try and stop her.

Fortunately, she'd owned her car. She swiftly carried the suitcase down the stairs and put it in the trunk. Then she hurried back for her laptop and music player.

She heard the water shut off. He'd be in there for the next few minutes. She had to hurry. Her hand on the door knob, she stopped and looked around the small apartment for the last time.

Then, taking a deep breath, she headed down the stairs and climbed in the car. She glanced up. He stood peering out the window, motioning to her to come back. Without hesitation she turned the key, shifted into drive and pulled away from the curb.

To the Reader

Using the Strategy of the Lotus Sutra

Many times when faced with a problem, you don't know what you need to do to solve it. Most of us have been taught to think about the situation to try and figure it out. If it has been an ongoing concern, your old behavior patterns have not been effective, and you don't know how to change them to end up with a more successful outcome. You may not understand the underlying core of the problem. It is too close, as it originates in you. Remember the principle of oneness of self and the environment. Everything in your life comes from the inside, to manifest in the outside world.

New practitioners tend to follow their habitual lifetime training. Experienced practitioners know that trying to figure it out first means you are trying to solve the problem backward. Instead they go to the Gohonzon first, thereby practicing the Strategy of the Lotus Sutra.

> *"Employ the strategy of the Lotus Sutra before any other."*
> Writings of Nichiren Daishonin, p. 1,246

This simply means to chant about your situation before trying to figure it out mentally.

Chanting before strategizing will feel strange at the beginning. You won't really believe you have access to everything you need inside of yourself. However, when you align yourself with the rhythm of the universe and access your higher wisdom and compassion, then you won't be deadlocked and will be able to resolve the situation in a manner which will permit you to take the next step toward happiness.

Let's see how this worked with Nancy. Initially, she did what a new practitioner usually does. She tried to figure out what to do while lying in bed and came away without any resolution.

She didn't achieve any clarity until she chanted about the problem and saw the whole picture—that Doug had a problem, that she couldn't change him, that her life and by extension her baby's life were going downhill with him, and that she could choose to live in the higher rather than in the lower worlds. She saw that her training had prepared her to live with the problem rather than taking steps to create happiness for herself, and that she was contributing to the problem by tolerating hurtful behavior from Doug.

Armed with this overview, when Doug came in and blamed her for his drinking, she saw that he was still in denial, that he owned the problem. She didn't want to wait for Doug to change, what with the baby coming, so she made the decision to leave him and go on with her life.

That decision could result in Doug's continuing to go downhill. According to Alcoholics Anonymous, an alcoholic usually has to hit bottom before being willing to address the problem. Life may be harder for Doug in the short run, if he persists in denial. For the long run, the most compassionate decision Nancy can make is to stop contributing to the problem and let Doug handle it himself.

Regardless of what happens to Doug, Nancy's life and the baby's life are going to improve.

On an emotional level, taking a big step such as this can be frightening, even when you know you are doing the right thing. Big changes can feel overwhelming. In order to combat this, you would do well to chant about each interim step as it comes up before taking action. This will help to break the change into bite-sized pieces which won't seem so overwhelming.

> "By wholeheartedly and directly meeting life's challenges, we bring forth from within ourselves the three bodies of the Buddha, which are truth, wisdom and compassion. The light of this internal wisdom constantly encourages and guides us toward true and correct action."
>
> Daisaku Ikeda, sBuddhism Day by Day, p. 245

By practicing the strategy of the Lotus Sutra—chanting first to access your higher wisdom and then taking action—your actions will assume a progressive character and the trajectory of your life will move in the direction of Buddhahood and unshakeable happiness.

26

Steps of Human Revolution

When Nancy knocked, her sister Sara opened the door. Her eyes widened as they flitted to Nancy's suitcase and back up to her sister's face.. "You've left him! You've left Doug!"

Nancy nodded. "He came home after a major bender. You should have seen him, dirty, smelling of liquor. He looked like a bum. I just can't live with his drinking anymore, so I'm leaving."

Her sister hugged her. "Are you okay?"

Nancy hugged her back. "I'm fine, but I need a place to land until I figure out what to do. Can I stay with you?"

Sara hesitated for a moment, and then opened the door wider, taking Nancy's suitcase. "I'll talk to Troy about it. How long do you think you'll be here?" As she started down the hall, she turned around briefly. "By the way, Mom's here." She went to look for Troy before Nancy could answer.

Nancy's heart sank. That was all she needed right now, to have to deal with her mother. Mom was not going to like what she'd done. She shook herself mentally. She had to look on the positive side. At least she had some breathing room to sort out what to do next.

Her sister returned with a towel and wash cloth. Her mother followed right on her heels.

After her mother kissed Nancy's cheek, she settled on the bed. "You're pregnant? And, you're going to leave Doug?"

She always got right to the point, Nancy thought with a sigh.

Nancy's mother looked at her intently. "If you don't have a husband, you'll have to work. Who'll take care of the baby?"

Nancy said, "I'll have to work that out. But I think it's better than staying." She paused. "Doug's drinking more and more and it's causing real problems."

Her mother frowned. "Do you make enough money to support a child?"

Nancy clenched her jaw, dodging her mother's question about her income. "Doug isn't ready to deal with his drinking and I won't live with it."

Sara intervened, putting a hand on her mother's shoulder. "It sounds as though his drinking has gotten pretty bad, Mom. I'm not sure the baby would be safe."

Her mother ignored Sara's comment. "I still think it's up to you to make the relationship work."

Nancy felt defensive, crossed her arms across her chest and tilted her chin. "I've heard that all my life. You've been unhappy because you've always put up with Dad's stuff."

Her mother flushed. "Whether I've been happy or unhappy has nothing to do with you. How would it have been for you and your sister if I'd left your father? I stayed because of you two, but I guess you never knew that."

Dead silence. Nancy looked at Sara. She had the same shocked look on her face that Nancy knew reflected on her own. "That explains everything," said Nancy. "No wonder you've always been so adamant about what women should do."

Gently she put her arm around her mother drawing her close. She had a lump in her throat. "I never understood why you stayed, when the two of you didn't seem happy together."

Her mother stepped back. "You knew that? I thought I'd hidden it from you."

Both Nancy and Sara nodded. "Once we were old enough to understand," Sara said, "we knew you were miserable."

"There's a difference between your situation and mine," persisted Nancy. She wanted her mother to understand why she wasn't going to repeat what she'd done.

"We had a father who was kind to us. You didn't have to worry about abuse. In my case, if Doug continues to go downhill, the cost could be the baby's safety. Doug has a scary temper and I'm afraid of him."

Nancy felt guilty at her mother's sad look but knew she'd made the right decision. "It was hard to make the decision, Mom. Please respect it, don't second-guess it. You've never lived with an alcoholic. It's a completely different situation."

Sara and her mother both wore puzzled expressions, as though they didn't know her.

"I'm afraid life is going to be very hard for you as a single parent," her mother said. "I don't want that for you."

Nancy's heart went out to her mother. "It may be," agreed Nancy. "But I still think it will be better than living with Doug's drinking and his temper."

"You've changed," said Sara.

Nancy nodded with determination. "I've finally taken charge of my life. I'll take what you think into account, but I'm making the decisions for my life."

Her mother pressed her lips together and walked out of the room. Sara flashed Nancy a reproving look and followed their mother.

Nancy wished she hadn't had to cut her mother off. *What's gotten into me?* She wasn't sure if she liked her new self either. Yet, she felt so much stronger. She was glad her sister was more flexible than her mother. At least Sara could see there were ligitimate problems. She rehashed the conversation in her head. The core of the disagreement stood out.

Her mother believed that women should always put themselves second no matter what. Nancy no longer believed that. She had a right to happiness for herself, not the obligation to make other people happy no matter what the cost. That included her sister and her parents. She had finally taken the reins of her life in her own hands, rather than waiting for the approval of someone else. She felt liberated.

She opened her suitcase and pulled out her shirts and pants, slipping them on hangers in the closet. She wanted to touch base with Hanako and Lisa and tell them that she had left Doug.

As she finished unpacking, she felt bone-tired. She'd never felt so exhausted. She stretched out on the chaise lounge in the corner and closed her eyes. She knew why her energy had departed. She'd been under enormous tension trying to handle her life with Doug. Now, for the moment, she was safe. She could finally relax.

Sleep was just creeping over her when she felt a soft flutter of movement in her abdomen. Her eyes flew open, her whole body alert and listening. There it was again, just like a little gas bubble. Her heart leapt. It was her baby! It had moved!

She'd known that she was pregnant but now, for the first time, she really believed there was a living baby inside her. A rush of joy filled her and then a feeling of protectiveness so strong it shocked her. She'd made the right decision. She wanted her baby born into a family which would love and protect it, not one where there were major problems wearing her down, distracting her attention. She relaxed, eagerly anticipating the little movement again.

She'd find an apartment as soon as she could. It was time to nest, make a home for herself. She was turning into a family. Anxiety blindsided her. *I am doing this alone!* What if her mother was right and she was kidding herself? After all, she'd never done this before. Maybe she *had* made a mistake.

She breathed a couple of Nam-myoho-renge-kyos. She gradually relaxed, the tension ebbing away. She'd already proven to herself that she could overcome obstacles with the practice. She'd be able to handle this too. She quickly recalled the promises, that the prayers of the practitioners would be answered, that anything could be achieved with the Mystic Law as the foundation. She had read the promises at every opportunity.

She felt sleep creep over her. Tomorrow was another day. She quickly fell asleep, a smile curving her lips.

To the Reader

Taking Your Life Into Your Hands

Nancy has not only been changing the way she behaves in her relationship with Doug, she is also doing it with her family of origin.

We are seeing, once again, how people resist when someone close to them tries to make changes. When a person starts to shift their behavior, other people close to them will try to get them to do what they've always done. This is the nature of things. If Nancy is persistent, her mother and sister will eventually accept her and her new way of being. But she is going to have to show them she can do it. That will be her next step.

The steps to accomplishing your human revolution occur one at a time. You chant about an issue and receive some ideas on what to do about it. Or, perhaps your attitude gradually changes. To have a situation change, we must change ourselves. Remember the principle of oneness of self and the environment.

One practitioner was having a relationship issue with her daughter. Their relationship had become so difficult that, after a particularly stressful visit, the mother had resolved not to visit her daughter again. After starting the practice she chanted about this relationship quite often. Gradually, without her even realizing what was happening, she relinquished her attempts to control the behavior of her daughter, letting go of the behaviors which had distressed her before. Once that happened, her daughter started to treat her mother differently and within a year or so they both were enjoying a much improved relationship.

Nancy is taking her life into her hands step by step, rather than continuing to accommodate whatever other people want her to do. This is a difficult thing to do, as all of her life experience would have led her in the other direction. She has to let go of her habitual beliefs and assert her right to live her life. These kinds of challenges are why consistent chanting and talking with other people are important for support.

There are three legs to doing human revolution. In the first leg, the steps of each person's human revolution occur through the process of chanting and resolving one obstacle and then another. With each encounter, you change in order to overcome the obstacle.

The second leg is to study, to deepen your understanding and experience of Buddhism through study and continuing to chant.

Then, the third leg of the process begins. At some point—and it is different for every person—you'll come to want to help other people find happiness in their lives as you have. As you overcome the obstacles in your own life, and then help others to do the same, your life will transform and you will become absolutely happy.

27

A Crucial Moment

When she awoke the next morning, Nancy felt disorientated. She didn't recognize the room. She looked around perplexed. *Where am I?* Then everything which had happened yesterday flooded back with a rush. Adrenalin shot through her. She had so many things to do and so little time. She only had a few months before the baby arrived.

The most important thing was to put herself in a position to make more money. Her mother had been right. She didn't make enough to support herself and the baby. For a moment, she felt anxious and then reminded herself that she had the practice and she could chant for what she needed.

Suiting her action to the thought, she placed her focal point on the wall and settled into a comfortable chair.

She had just begun the chant when there was a knock on the door and Sara poked her head in. "I thought you might want breakfast," she paused, watching Nancy. "What are you doing?"

Nancy felt disrupted. It wasn't like being at home, where she could keep her environment the way she wanted. "I'm chanting. Just give me fifteen minutes, then I'll come and help you with breakfast."

With a final curious look, Sara shut the door quietly.

Nancy settled herself again. How had Hanako taught her to chant? Oh yes, she'd told her to be specific and chant for what she wanted.

She thought for a moment. How much money a year did she need to be comfortable? She'd need to pay for rent and health insurance. She'd need to maintain the car, food, doctor bills. It would probably come to $40,000 a year. That seemed like a lot, almost impossible. It was $15,000 more than she was making now! It seemed so odd to be chanting for something as unspiritual as money. For a moment, she felt overwhelmed by the magnitude of what she had to do.

She could hear Hanako say, "Never dwell on what you don't want. Remember your thoughts and actions create causes for your future." Nancy didn't want to fail in this, so she reminded herself to redirect her mind away from her fears and keep her attention on successfully achieving her goal of $40,000. She refocused herself, repeating Nam-myoho-renge -kyo softly to herself.

"Set your goal and don't try to figure out how you'll get there," Hanako had said. "Let the universe work it out. Most of the time you have no idea the best way for it to come about." Since Nancy couldn't see any way to make the $40,000, that seemed like very good advice. It felt uncomfortable, though. She was so used to trying to figure out how to resolve a problem.

As always, she could feel the shift when she settled into chanting. Calmness and a feeling of strength came over her. Then the thoughts began to flow, thoughts she would never have had otherwise. It always felt as though she'd tapped into a higher wisdom with more breadth and depth than her ordinary thinking.

She reflected on her past job experience with the recycling center, where she'd supervised a couple of people. That experience taught her how to set up a work flow and how to handle customers. She couldn't help but notice that the front desk staff where she worked now seemed more concerned about getting paperwork done than welcoming clients. The whole atmosphere was cold and unwelcoming. This seemed wrong to Nancy. The agency clients had mental health problems and needed to feel that they'd come to a place where people cared about them.

Until now, Nancy had only made casual observations. She hadn't considered the office part of her job. But now, as she chanted, she found herself looking at the situation from an overview, as though she were personally responsible for running it.

She reached over to the table and picked up a pen and paper to make notes.

Thoughts flowed. The front desk needed two people, one to welcome clients and the other to take care of the insurance paperwork. Each employee should be trained in how to handle the phones so they were consistent in giving out the same information. They needed to set up a system for distributing the data entry work, so that everyone was busy but not overwhelmed. She shifted on the chair as she noted these ideas.

The waiting room should be welcoming. They could paint the walls a cheerful color. Having current magazines and maybe a CD player with some music might help too. Another note.

She resolved to write a proposal to give to Sue, the outpatient program director. Nancy smiled. She really liked Sue. She was so approachable. She respected her too. Sue didn't miss much going on with the therapists and staff in her department, and she addressed issues right up front.

Nancy knew she was taking a risk by going around Annette. But Annette was the problem here. It was common knowledge that if you took a proposal to her, Annette would either suppress it, or convince Sue that it was all her own idea. That wouldn't help Nancy get ahead.

Since Nancy had made the decision to be competent at work, Sue had complimented her more than once on her efficiency and her output. Writing a proposal would take their relationship to another level. She'd have to stay late to do it, but she couldn't see any other way to create additional value in her job.

Chanting, she felt both comforted and energized. When she finished, her whole day had come into order and she knew exactly how to proceed. With a final, slow Nam-myoho-renge-kyo, she stood up slowly, reorientating herself to the day. Time to help Sara with breakfast.

The next day, during slow periods, Nancy worked on the proposal. Anxiety arose as she contemplated how Annette would react. She decided she couldn't worry about Annette. Nancy continued to write down her ideas. By the time the proposal was complete it was seven o'clock. Every one had gone home.

As she worked the kinks out of her shoulders, she was tired but ready, even a little excited. It felt good to look at the office and analyze what changes were needed to smooth its operation. Having a challenge certainly made working more interesting. She was amazed she was even writing this proposal. She never would have taken this on six months ago. She felt satisfied as she closed the front door, a good work day.

The next morning chanting helped to settle her nerves as she faced taking the proposal to Sue. Now that it was time to speak up, she was more worried about Annette's reaction. Once she gave Sue the proposal, Nancy would have stepped squarely onto Annette's turf.

Nancy thought of Annette as a moody perfectionist. If crossed, she could be vindictive and nasty. Nancy had also noticed that Annette seemed to be in pain fairly frequently, walked with a limp and used a cane. Annette always seemed to present her good side to Sue, while treating other people with an underlying disrespect.

Nancy hesitated. Maybe she'd be in serious trouble if she went in to see Sue. Annette's desk was close to Sue's door, so she'd notice Nancy going into her office. She hoped Annette wouldn't take it out on her. After all, she was her supervisor.

Then Nancy felt that inner strength coming to the fore. In the past she hadn't wanted to make Annette angry or cause waves, but now she had to look out for the baby's future by doing the best work she could. She had to speak up if she wanted to advance up the ladder. *Annette's had her chance and she hasn't done a good job. Now it's my turn.*

At ten, she saw that Sue's door was open. Proposal in hand, Nancy knocked softly. Sue looked up and a smile lit her face. "Come in." Nancy closed the door.

She liked Sue's casual clothes and informal ways. Her office felt welcoming. She'd set up a seating area where three people could talk and her desk faced the wall. Nancy noted that it was very different from Annette's office where the desk was in the power position, right in the middle of the floor facing the door. Where Annette had a single straight-backed chair beside her desk Sue offered visitors comfortable upholstered chairs. Nancy gratefully sank into one.

She returned Sue's friendly gaze, hesitated a moment, then screwed up her courage. "I've had some thoughts on how we might make the front office more efficient and also more welcoming to clients," she began.

Sue said, "Wonderful. Let's hear your ideas."

Nancy settled herself. "This is a mental health agency. I'm concerned about the atmosphere in the front office when people come in. It feels cold, and our staff seems to care more about getting the paperwork done than greeting the clients."

Sue nodded. "I've noticed that too."

"I've put together some suggestions on possible changes." Nancy picked up her proposal.

Sue took it and started reading. After a few moments she nodded and smiled. "This is very interesting," she said. "You've thought a lot about this."

Chanted about it, thought Nancy. *I hadn't thought about it until I chanted about it.*

Sue said, "You have some good ideas here. Let me think about them for a couple of days. I've been thinking about the front office too and you have a different and interesting way of looking at it." It was a dismissal and Nancy stood to go.

As she opened the door, Annette stared directly at Nancy. Her face tightened and she gave her a swift, calculating look. She looked sleek and well-groomed, her dark hair pulled smoothly back. Her steel grey suit skimmed closely to her body, with a red scarf around her neck. It complimented her fair skin and dark hair, but Nancy couldn't help thinking she looked like a wounded shark.

Uh-oh. Nancy felt chilled and shivered. She was afraid she'd made an enemy. Mentally she shook herself. If Annette didn't like what Nancy had done, too bad. She was doing it for the baby. Remembering the practice, she felt comforted as she went back to her work station.

After work that evening, Nancy called Hanako.

"I chanted to understand my life with Doug and once I did, I decided I couldn't stay," she said. "Doug's drinking has gotten out of hand. I've left him."

"I'm not surprised," Hanako responded. "I didn't think you'd be happy in that relationship."

Nancy then briefly described the situation with Annette at the office. "I'm not quite sure how to chant about this."

Hanako was silent for a moment. "I'd chant for your success with the project and for Annette's happiness. After all, she wouldn't be behaving this way if she were happy."

That made sense to Nancy. She'd thought more than once that Annette wasn't happy.

"I would also chant for your protection every morning."

Nancy shivered. "If you could have seen the look she gave me. It gave me the willies."

"Using your practice, you'll be able to handle whatever comes up," Hanako said.

Nancy felt better hearing the confidence in Hanako's voice. "Thanks. I'll start this evening."

That evening back at Sara's, Nancy closed the door and settled down to chant. She didn't like Annette. At first it was a struggle to chant for her happiness. But, then she remembered what Hanako had said. People don't behave in negative ways if they're happy.

Nancy began to chant with more conviction. She chanted for the success of the proposal and that her ideas would benefit the people and clients in the front office. Finally she chanted for her own protection. When she ended a half hour later, she felt satisfied and complete. It had been a good day, a new beginning.

To the Reader

Chanting in a Crucial Moment

There are times in our lives when we come up against a crucial moment, such as a diagnosis of cancer. Another might be if you were divorced and your ex-spouse tried to get exclusive custody of your child. Although Nancy's crucial moment is not quite as dramatic, what happens in her work life is going to directly impact the quality of life she will have with her child.

In the case of someone facing a diagnosis of cancer, the natural thing would be to chant to be rid of cancer. But chanting in this way is negative, because it acknowledges the cancer.

An experienced practitioner will sit in front of the Go-honzon, firmly clarify what they *do* want, and then chant with focus and intensity for that goal. In the case of a cancer diagnosis, you would chant for good health rather than to get rid of the cancer.

Chanting in this manner is not just a reaction to the circumstance. Chanting in a crucial moment is proactive with a clear destination in mind. A practitioner might chant in this manner for as long as it takes. Parents have been known to chant for hours and hours over the serious illness of a child. However long, continue chanting until you feel deep inside that your concern has been resolved. You will feel a sense of relaxation, as though you don't have to worry any more. This is not just an internal shift. You will find that the outward circumstances have been resolved as well.

> *"Struggling against great difficulty enables us to develop ourselves tremendously. We call forth and manifest those abilities dormant within us. Difficulty can then be a source of dynamic new growth and progress."*
>
> Daisaku Ikeda, *Faith Into Action,* p. 107

Jocelyn, a brand new practitioner, was diagnosed with a brain tumor a couple of months after she started to practice. Her doctor described the tumor as having seven connections in the brain and that it would be a ten hour operation to remove it.

A more experienced member, who had seen many other people overcome cancer, told Jocelyn she needed to chant three hours a day. Jocelyn was non-plussed. She was working full time. How could she fit it in three hours of chanting? Her advisor told her she could break down the chanting time into fifteen minute, or half hour segments, but that this was a crucial moment and she needed to mount an all-out assault on the cancer.

Although it was hard, Jocelyn determined to chant the three hours a day for full recovery. By the time of the surgery, three months later, the surgeon discovered only one connection remained between the tumor and her brain. It was easily removed in a one hour long operation. There has been no recurrence, twenty five years later.

Nancy must take a proactive stance to break through the inhibitions, which have held her back from taking the actions necessary to advancing her career. We saw her attitude shift, as she began to contemplate the changes needed in the front office. But she still must address her fears, both to make the presentation to Sue and about

Annette's response. As she chants and prays proactively and with focus, her life condition will respond and she will develop the confidence and determination to take the actions necessary to move her career forward.

How to Chant in a Crucial Moment

- Clarify what you want to have happen.
- Make sure you are chanting for a positive goal, not for what you don't want. For example, chant for health, not to get rid of disease.
- Chant for however long it takes until you have a feeling that the issue is resolved.

28

Make a Determination to Win

The next morning, Nancy looked up from her desk. Annette had barely hung up her coat and had gone directly into Sue's office. Annette's limp was more pronounced today. Were they discussing Nancy's proposal? She was glad she'd chanted for protection this morning. She might need it.

In a half an hour, Annette came out frowning and turned into her office. She swung her cane as though she'd like to hit someone. In a few moments her phone rang. "I'd like to see you in my office," Annette said in a brusque tone. "Now."

Nancy's anxiety skyrocketed. *She's angry. What am I going to say when she asks me why I didn't bring the proposal to her first?* She slowly walked to Annette's office.

Annette motioned her to the straight, uncomfortable chair by her desk. She wasn't smiling. Her eyes narrowed when she said, "I understand you took Sue a proposal on how to change the front office." This was not a question.

Nancy nodded. "That's right."

Annette leaned forward with a penetrating look. "I'm your supervisor. Don't go over my head without talking to me first," she snapped. Nancy froze. She didn't know what to say without putting her foot into it further.

"Well? What do you have to say?"

Nancy felt flustered. "I'm sorry if I upset you." *But I never would have taken that proposal to you first.* Her anxiety heightened.

"I'm warning you. I can't have someone working for me who is insubordinate. I expect you to bring me everything first." She hit her palm on the desk. "Let's see your proposal." At that moment, Nancy felt the baby kick. She had to hold on to her job.

She dropped her gaze and quietly said, "Of course. I'll get an extra copy to you right away."

Annette nodded and Nancy went back to her office to do as she'd been asked. What would she do if she lost this job? She'd better not upset Annette any more than she already had. Nothing more was said as Tuesday passed, then Wednesday. Nancy battled with her tension.

Late Wednesday, Annette came by her cubicle with a stack of reports to be typed. When she brought her another stack the next morning, Nancy felt frantic. There wasn't enough time to do this additional work on top of her regular duties. All at once it hit her. Annette was trying to get back at her for going over her head. She started to panic, but then reminded herself: *You can do this: pull yourself together.*

As the daylight faded, she had completed little more than half the work that Annette had given her.

As she looked through the remaining stack of work preparing for the next day, she noticed a work order clipped to a year-end report and the figures to go with it. There was no due date on the order. She walked to Annette's office to ask her, but found the door was closed, the lights off. She sighed and turned away. *I'll talk to her in the morning.*

That evening when Nancy went home she spent nearly an hour chanting. She felt that sense of being connected and a sense of strength and confidence came over her.

The underlying tension between her and Annette didn't bode well. She reflected that it must be hard for Annette with that bum leg. She wished she wasn't so nasty. Although she chanted through gritted teeth, she forced herself to chant for Annette's happiness and for her own protection. She resolved this situation would work out and she would keep her job.

She debated letting go of the proposal. Maybe it wasn't worth being on Annette's bad side. Then there was a shift and she seemed to see the whole situation from an overview. She would fail if she gave up half-way and wouldn't be able to move up in the organization. She could remember that Hanako had told her never to give up half-way, but to chant until you got your goal. Nancy straightened her back and made a determination to see it through no matter what. Instead of giving up on the proposal, she chanted instead for its success.

At nine the next morning, Annette called her into her office again. She looked as sleek as ever. How could she be both so beautiful and so vindictive? Nancy thought.

Annette was terse. "Where is the year-end report and the work sheet that goes with it?"

"I've been working on them but I'm not finished yet."

"What?" Annette peered at Nancy over her designer glasses. "You knew they need to be finished by noon."

Nancy looked at her aghast. She was furious. *Annette's impossible!* "You didn't tell me when they were due. You know you didn't. The year-end report is seventy pages!" She felt the beginnings of panic.

Annette's face had hardened and now she fixed her to the wall with a look like a dagger. "If you can't do it, I'll find someone who can."

It hit her. This was it! Annette was setting her up to fail. Nancy once again drew upon that quiet strength that chanting had given her. She looked Annette in the eye. "I'll get it to you by 12:30."

Nancy was absolutely not going to let Annette get away with this. She knew she was in a battle for her reputation and her job. She could feel the strength inside. She quickly returned to her desk, chanting Nam-myo-ho-renge-kyo under her breath. She determined she was going to meet the deadline, no matter what. Her fingers flew. At the two-hour mark, her shoulders ached and her neck felt as though the tendons were encased in iron. At lunch time she continued typing without pause. Finally, she typed the last sentence. She took the report into Annette and firmly set it on her desk—12:28 p.m.

"Here it is."

"Better late than never." Annette looked disappointed. "Where are the figures?"

Exhausted, Nancy felt both angry and terrified. "I'm still working on them."

Annette couldn't conceal the victorious look that flashed over her face. "They're due for the board meeting at one p.m.," she said coldly. Nancy felt as though she'd been blindsided. She could imagine all the board members being told about her incompetency. She flushed, even though she tried not to.

Annette sniffed. "You've let us all down." She picked up the year-end report and went to Sue's office.

Nancy watched her go. What was Annette going to say to Sue, when she asked why the report wasn't finished? Discouragement settled over her. She felt desperate. The baby kicked again. She just couldn't lose this job! Would the ax fall after the board meeting?

When the meeting ended, Sue called Nancy into her office. Sue's blue pantsuit accented her blue eyes and blonde, curly hair. Sue usually dressed more casually. The meeting must have been important. Nancy tensed.

Sue settled in her chair, crossed her legs, and in her usual forthright manner asked, "What happened to you today? Usually you're on top of things."

"I agree. But since Annette found out I'd taken the proposal to you without running it by her, she's given me lots of extra work. She didn't tell me when the report and the figures were due."

Sue frowned, "You didn't know when they were due?"

"That's right," said Nancy quietly. "I have the work order she gave me." Sue sat silently for a moment, her chin on her hand. "I'd like to see it." Nancy felt a shock. She's not sure I'm telling the truth, she thought with apprehension.

The two of them crossed the floor, past the cubicles of the other team members, to Nancy's desk. She handed Sue the incomplete order. Sue glanced over it quickly. Her co-workers watched as they passed. Nancy felt her face burn.

Sue closed her office door. "Why didn't you go to Annette first about the proposal?" Nancy decided to level with Sue and was relieved Annette couldn't overhear the conversation

Nancy took a deep breath. Her job was on the line. "For a number of reasons, but mainly that Annette's been in charge of the front office and I didn't think she'd appreciate me having other ideas."

Sue seemed to be remembering something for a moment. She refocused on Nancy. "You had other reasons, too?"

Nancy nodded. "I don't like having to say this, but I've seen her take resentments out on people before."

Sue cocked her head. "And?"

Nancy hesitated, then remembered Sue had always been trustworthy and dealt with issues up front. She could only do the same.

"I've also seen her take credit for things other people have done, and I didn't want her doing that with this proposal," Nancy said in a rush.

"I see," said Sue slowly. "Thanks for being frank with me."

Nancy felt relieved. She'd finally told Sue the truth of what was happening on the team. She didn't know where it would go, but at least she'd let Sue know.

Over the weekend, Nancy chanted longer and harder that Sue would implement the proposal and, above all, that she would keep her job. Angry as she'd been with Annette, the more she chanted for her supervisor's happiness, the less anger welled up inside. She didn't wish Annette ill anymore. She finished the session feeling more determined. She was not going to let Annette run over her.

To the Reader

Handling a Difficult Person

We have just seen Nancy in a battle for her livelihood with a difficult adversary. The temptation, when faced with something like this, is to fight and possibly take revenge. When you're tempted, remember the law of cause and effect.

When you take an action, for good or for ill, you are creating a seed which will manifest in your future. You don't want to become reactive and fall into the lower worlds. Resist temptation to take an action that will create a problem sometime later. You always want to respond in a proactive manner that will create positive causes. The following example will illustrate.

A woman left her drug-addicted husband. He was a vindictive person, and could be a bad enemy. A practitioner advised her always to act in an impeccable fashion, as he would use any slip against her. As the months, then several years went by, she did exactly that, always living up to her highest standards. As had been predicted, he tried to use anything he could against her, but somehow nothing he tried to do produced any negative effect in her circumstances. She ended up moving into a much higher position in another city. She became happy in her life.

Had she become embroiled in a fight with him, the whole negative situation would undoubtedly have gone further downhill and she wouldn't have been in a position to move on when the time came. Nancy is chanting for

Annette's happiness. This is difficult to do considering the circumstances. Remembering the law of cause and effect, Nancy doesn't want to chant for anything negative to happen to Annette.

Yet, Nancy *does* chant for her own protection. This is always valuable and unmistakably provides an invisible yet effective protective umbrella. She also made the determination that she wasn't going to let Annette get the best of her. In other words, she wasn't going to succumb to Annette's negative scenario. Nancy is doing everything she can to perform at her best.

Nancy was also honest and truthful with Sue. She didn't try to hurt Annette, but she told Sue what had happened thus providing her director with insight into the dynamics of the team. Annette's own actions over time led to this discussion and provide an example of the law of cause and effect in action.

When handling difficult people, you want to first make sure that your own actions live up to the highest standard. You don't want to become vengeful or combative. Keep your eye on the positive outcome you want. Chant for the way you want the situation to work out and let the universe handle how this will occur.

When you chant, you don't have to fight someone who is being difficult. You want to chant for their happiness and, if you think there is danger to you for your own protection. Finally make a determination that you are not going to give in to negativity and follow it up with whatever actions are required.

How to Handle a Difficult Person

- Chant for his or her happiness.
- Chant for the resolution you want.
- Act on any ideas you receive which would help resolve the situation.
- Chant for your own protection.
- Behave according to your highest standards.
- Remember the law of cause and effect.

29

You are a Buddha, Not a Beggar

Monday morning, Nancy started the day by heading for the filing cabinets outside Sue's office. She needed to file all the extra work from the week before. Soon after she'd begun, she felt the air swirl as Annette swept past her and turned into Sue's office. A few minutes later, Nancy heard voices being raised and recognized one of them as Annette's. She wondered what was being said.

Fifteen minutes later, the door to Sue's office opened with a bang, hitting the wall. Annette stormed out, her cane swinging, her face flaming. She spied Nancy and shot her a venomous look. The woman went as quickly as she could to her own office, grabbed her belongings and slammed out the front door.

All the team members within earshot raised their heads with inquiring looks. Nancy shrugged as if she didn't know what was going on. But she was afraid she did.

She finished the filing and returned to her desk.

Later that morning, Sue called a team meeting. Nancy entered the conference room with the others. She looked around the room. Annette was conspicuously absent.

Sue looked tired and drawn but took the lead. Nancy thought Sue must be under a lot of stress. Her boss hesitated then said, "I called this meeting so I could talk with all of you at once." She looked down, clearly gathering herself and then looked up at them again. "I regret having to tell you that I've had to let Annette go." The team members murmured and looked at each other as they absorbed the implications. Annette had supervised four of them, including Nancy.

Momentarily, Nancy was horrified. Was it her fault after what she'd told Sue? Then she felt great relief sweep over her. She felt safe, as though a threat had just been removed, not just from her but from the other team members too.

Sue continued. "I'll be hiring someone to take her place. I'll keep you all appraised of the status of the hiring process." Sue looked around at each person. "It's important that we don't let this affect our clients." Everyone nodded. Sue stood and the team members returned back to their desks.

Nancy was sure Annette's firing was her fault. She really needed to chant for Annette's happiness now. Her stomach roiled with a sick feeling combined with relief.

She called Hanako. Just hearing her voice made her feel better. Nancy brought her quickly up to date. "I didn't want this to happen. I feel as though it was my fault Annette was fired because of what I said to Sue." She paced as she talked.

Hanako asked, "You told the truth didn't you?"

Nancy nodded and then realized that Hanako couldn't see her over the phone. "Of course."

"Then her firing was the result of her own actions, not your fault," Hanako said firmly. "Remember the simultaneity of cause and effect? She set the seeds for her own future in her own past actions."

Nancy's mind raced. So this is what the practitioners meant, when they talked about the law of cause and effect. This wasn't theory, but worked itself out in everyday life. She'd found a key to making her life better. She would need to watch what she did, so she would create the kind of causes that would lead to a happier life.

She pulled her attention back to the conversation. "I'm continuing to chant for her happiness," said Nancy.

Hanako agreed. "You should. At some point, you're going to know what happened to her"

"Thanks Hanako," Nancy said. "I feel better after talking to you."

"Any time. You know that."

That night, Nancy fell asleep quickly, without the enormous feeling of guilt she'd been carrying. She resolved to talk to Sue the next day to make sure Hanako was right.

First thing the next morning she knocked on Sue's door. Sue looked up inquiringly.

Nancy said, "Could I have a word with you?"

Sue beckoned her in. Nancy closed the door behind her.

She felt a little breathless. "I want to know if Annette was fired because of what I told you."

Sue said, "Actually it was a number of things. By law I can't discuss the reasons with you, but what she did to you was the final straw. That was not good for the team." Sue had protected the team members, thought Nancy. Her respect for Sue grew.

A great wave of relief swept over Nancy. Annette was gone and it wasn't her fault she'd been fired. She took a deep breath and then realized with a jolt that Annette's leaving left a job opening.

With Annette gone only a short while, Nancy felt a bit embarrassed at being so eager. But here was her opportunity. "I'd like to apply for the job."

Sue's smile lit up her face and the drawn look vanished. "Go to Human Resources and talk with Becky. She'll get you an application."

As Nancy got up to go back to her desk, Sue said, "We'll need to post the position outside the agency, as well as in-house."

Nancy said, "I understand." At least Sue hadn't discouraged her. She'd even seemed pleased.

Nancy walked out of Sue's office. If she got the position, she'd probably achieve her goal of making enough money to support the baby. Her hopes lifted. When she went to get the application, she'd ask how much the job paid.

With a mounting sense of excitement, she realized it was time to chant for her new goal in addition to the others.

To the Reader

Understanding Cause and Effect

You are watching Nancy turn her life around. She is now using the practice to handle problems. She's laying a positive foundation for her life, using ideas that come to her while she chants and taps into her Buddha nature.

These ideas have come from the highest part of her and have directed her onto a progressive path which is moving her in the direction of happiness.

You have seen her begin to use abilities which she really enjoys, but which have been mostly hidden up until now. In order to do this she had to overcome her non-assertiveness, which kept her from speaking up. It stopped her from using those abilities to make contributions at work.

You have also seen her handle a very difficult person. Nancy remained positive without falling into the lower worlds. She rose to the challenge with Annette and she continued to chant for Annette's happiness even though Annette tried to get her fired. With this fundamental shift in attitude, Nancy is now using the law of cause and effect to create causes in her life that will build fortune in her life and lead to happiness.

The law of cause and effect is neutral. If a person makes negative causes with the intent to try to control and hurt other people, then that negativity will result in a gradual downhill spiral in the life of the person expressing it. Likewise, when a person stays positive and refuses to engage with the negativity of another person—chanting for their happiness and keeping their own behavior positive—their life will take an upward spiral. Fortune and happiness will grow in their experience.

You have now seen that when you use the practice to guide you, make the changes necessary and take the actions needed to move forward, life will take a progressive upward path. Anyone can do this, including you. Daily consistent chanting and using the strategy of the Lotus Sutra to handle problems will put you firmly on this path.

◢30◣

A Big Leap Takes Courage

First thing Monday morning, Nancy visited HR. She'd chanted all weekend about the job opening and although nervous, was determined to do her best to get it. She knew she might not have as much experience as other applicants, but she could present herself in the best light possible.

As she stepped in the back door, she could see the Human Resources sign down the hall. Becky, a trim dark haired thirty-five year-old, glanced up from her computer when Nancy tapped on the door. She swiveled around to face her.

Nancy smiled. "I've come to get an application for Supervisor I."

"So, you're going to go for it?"

Nancy nodded.

"Good for you." Becky's face lit up with a smile.

A little embarrassed, Nancy asked, "Can you tell me how much the job pays?"

"That's probably something you and Sue would work out, but it ranges from $37,500 to $45,000, depending on experience." Becky paused. "You do understand that we have to advertise outside the agency, don't you?"

"Yes, Sue told me." Nancy didn't know how this might affect her chances. She'd supervised a couple of people at the recycling agency but Annette had been responsible for four people. Sue was a good supervisor, so Nancy resolved to learn Sue's skills. Nancy smiled at Becky. "When will they close the applications?"

"We'll give it a couple of weeks. No one wants to leave that position empty too long." She handed Nancy a packet. "Here's the job description and application."

Nancy walked straight to her desk, the packet nearly burning her fingers. She was anxious to read the application and quickly she scanned it. There was some budgetary work. She didn't have much experience with that. She *had* gotten a grant, though. The position of Supervisor I was responsible for up to five people. At least she'd had some experience.

She'd have to think about how to present herself in the strongest way. The proposal wouldn't hurt her chances. She really hoped she'd have the chance to put her ideas into effect.

She felt her breathing speed up. This was a crucial moment. Her whole life could change. She wanted to chant with someone. She called Hanako.

Hanako was delighted and invited Nancy over. As she entered the now familiar room, warmth stole into her heart. *Hanako was such a good friend.*

Nancy explained what was happening.

Hanako said, "Just so we get the most out of our chanting, I want to remind you of a couple of things. Remember, there's a big difference between a hope and a determination. With a hope, you may not fully believe that your goal is possible, but hope for the best.

With a determination, there is no doubt you will make it happen, and you commit to take the necessary actions, so be specific about what you want."

Nancy nodded. She wasn't a beggar here but a Buddha in charge of her life. That was so different in this practice.

She turned to Hanako. "I want us to chant that I land this job and make at least $40,000 a year." She made the determination. She had to get it. She had a baby to support.

They turned to the Gohonzon and assumed the prayer position. Nancy reflected, while rubbing her beads together, that she held her life in her hands. It was up to her. She began to repeat Nam-myoho-renge-kyo.

Early on, Hanako had told her that she had eternal life force and wisdom within her and it was also in everything else in the universe. As she chanted and brought this to the fore, she would become a magnet for what she needed.

As she settled into the chant and felt that unification with the universal energy, she had the experience of looking her situation from an overview once again. She quickly reviewed her past work experience and then, with a start, realized she had forgotten to update her resume. She could see it would be a good idea to include all of her recycling experience. She'd had both office and supervisory experience there. She'd supervised two people as well as organizing volunteers and scheduling the work. She'd done some budgeting and she'd even written a grant and received it. She could feel herself become stronger and more confident. By the end of the chanting session she was enthusiastic about reworking her résumé.

Taking her leave, she gave Hanako a quick hug. "Thanks so much for supporting me."

"That's what we do for one another. You know that." Hanako smiled.

A lump came into Nancy's throat. "You're a wonderful friend." She turned and ran down the stairs to her car.

Once home, she made a cup of tea and sipped on it as she worked on the résumé. She felt strong and focused. By the end of the evening the résumé was finished. Before she went to bed, she filled out the application. She'd take the reworked résumé and application to Becky first thing in the morning.

The following week, Sue began to interview job applicants. Nancy could see Sue's door from her desk and, as she worked, she kept an eye on the people who went in and out. Some she didn't recognize. One was a woman in her fifty's and the other a young man, probably younger than she was. She wondered what kind of experience he'd had.

The second week, she nervously tried to decide whether being at the tail end of the applicants was a good or bad thing. She couldn't stop thinking about what was happening with the interviews. She realized she was getting obsessive about it. Even telling herself to settle down didn't calm her. Finally, at lunch, Sue asked her to come in the next day. All at once, she wanted more time.

When she went in for her interview Nancy had butterflies. Sue must have realized this, as she tried to put Nancy at her ease. "I was pleased when you said you wanted to apply," she said. "You showed real initiative when you brought me the proposal."

Nancy relaxed. She might have the inside track after all.

Sue quickly reviewed the résumé and then looked up. "What kind of supervisory experience did you have at the recycling agency?"

"There were four in the office and I supervised two of them. I planned the work load and made sure there were enough people to handle it. I worked with volunteers to make sure there was enough work for them to do, that they were scheduled properly and gave good customer service. I wrote a grant and got it, so I have some experience with budgets."

Nancy paused, considered her next statement and then said, "These are my strengths. I've worked here for three years and understand the agency, the organization and the people, so I can be up to speed quickly. I'm good with people and have experience on the front desk. I'm a quick learner and will want some training in supervision."

Sue sat back in her chair. "You've had some supervisory experience, and I like the fact you are willing to do whatever is necessary to develop the skills," she said. "I'll be in touch."

Nancy warmed. The interview had gone well.

As she walked back to her desk, thinking about the conversation with Sue, Nancy couldn't know how well she stacked up against the other applicants. Even so, she thought she might have a real chance.

Then she felt anxious. How would she handle this job with the baby coming? She didn't want to tell Sue she was pregnant until after her decision had been made. The agency did grant time off for new mothers. But would it be enough?

How could she spend the time she needed with the baby and also do good work for the agency? For a moment it seemed as though a hand closed around her heart. Maybe she'd taken on more than she could handle.

"One day at a time," she whispered to herself. "You can handle it one day at a time." *Remember the practice.*

To the Reader

Hope versus Determination

If you have been chanting for a goal for a while and there is no movement, it may be because you have been chanting with hope rather than determination. To chant with hope would mean that you hope for the best but don't really believe down deep that you can have what you want. There is that doubt that you really have a Buddha nature and can create your life as you wish it to be. When this is the case the universe will reflect your belief and there won't be any movement toward your goal.

Let's say you want to lose fifty pounds, a substantial amount of weight. You might chant to lose it but if you don't really believe it's possible, you probably won't follow up with the actions necessary to make your goal a reality.

When you chant with determination you are not a supplicant. You are a Buddha absolutely in charge of your life. So you chant with the attitude that it will be this way, no doubt. Ideas will show up showing you what you need to do to follow up with the actions necessary to accomplish your goal.

When you sit in front of the Gohonzon your life is literally in your hands. You can create it as you wish it. Remember that you have the universal life force and wisdom within that can attract anything you need to accomplish your goal.

You don't have to force anything. You just have to establish the intention, be willing to take any needed actions, and have confidence that the universe will provide the path.

As we can see in Nancy's case, when she made the determination to apply for the position that would allow her to support her baby, she then developed ideas regarding the front office. By chanting, she raised her life condition so she had the courage which allowed her to move forward toward her goal.

If your forward momentum has stalled, ask yourself, am I chanting with a hope or a determination?

31

One step at a Time

That evening after work, Nancy stretched out with a sigh of relief on the chaise lounge. She'd heard she'd have more energy in the second trimester but she hadn't seen it yet.

Her phone rang. She picked it up. "Yes?"

It was Doug. "Where are you Nancy?" he asked, a pleading note in his voice. "I need to see you. Let's talk things over." Nancy startled and felt apprehensive. Hearing his voice was like an electric jolt.

Oh no. I don't want to talk to Doug now. She knew she was going to have to make it clear that she'd decided to go on with her life without him. As tired as she was, talking with Doug was the last thing she wanted to do tonight. Still, it was probably better to get it over with. She could probably have the privacy to talk with him in the living room. Sara and Troy were playing cards with friends at the back of the house in the family room. Reluctantly, she told Doug he could come on over.

Nancy opened the door. Doug looked a lot better than he had the last time she'd seen him. He looked clean and groomed and his eyes weren't bloodshot. He reached out to hug her. Nancy stepped back. He dropped his arms, disappointment creasing his face.

"Aren't you even going to give me a hug?"

Nancy disregarded the question. "Come into the living room. We can talk in there."

They settled into two comfortable chairs. He leaned forward eagerly and cut right to the chase. "We belong together, Nancy."

Nancy shook her head. She didn't know that any more. What she knew now was that she was on her own. She didn't think she could rely on him and she wasn't going to set herself up.

"I don't think we can be together, Doug," she said gently. "Your drinking got out of control last week and it changed everything for me."

"But I haven't touched a drop since," he said quickly.

"Maybe not. But you will again, and when you do, it's going to be the same way. I don't want that kind of stress in my life. Look what happened the last time."

Doug looked embarrassed. "I won't let it happen again."

For a moment Nancy felt herself weakening. She took a deep breath. That inner strength came to the fore. "I guess I don't trust that," said Nancy. "I don't think you're willing to make the decision to stop drinking and I have to think of someone other than myself now. I have the baby to think of."

"But, how will you do it all by yourself?"

"I don't know," Nancy acknowledged. "But I'm moving in that direction."

Doug raised his voice. "You're being selfish and cutting me out of our child's life."

"I haven't said I was going to do anything of the sort," Nancy said. She did wonder how she was going to handle visits, if he didn't stop drinking.

"This is why I can't stay with you, Doug. You don't think about anyone but yourself."

His face turned red. "There you go again," he said with disgust.

Nancy stood up. "This conversation isn't getting us anywhere," she said. "I want you to leave now."

Doug looked at her with incredulity. "You're throwing me out?"

Nancy nodded and said firmly, "I don't want to, but I'm not going to keep on fighting."

She walked toward the outside door. Doug came with her, protesting the whole way. "You're not listening to me! This isn't right!"

Nancy sighed deeply. "I've heard enough to see that nothing has changed and it simply isn't going to work."

The door at the end of the hall opened and Sara stood there. "I thought I heard a ... Doug!" she exclaimed.

"Doug is just leaving," Nancy said firmly, giving her sister a meaningful glance. Nancy turned to Doug. "I hope you'll be happy." She started up the stairs to her room, leaving him hesitating in the doorway.

He glanced at Sara. She stood with arms crossed over her chest and didn't move. He shrugged, and shoulders slumped, he slowly walked down the steps.

To the Reader

Standing Strong Against the Eight Winds

When Nancy faced Doug's pleas to come back she could have been swayed by him. If she had allowed this to happen, she would have been responding from one of the lower Ten Worlds, where we react to our circumstances. In her past history with Doug, she would be influenced by his arguments and give in to him.

She would have been swayed by one of the eight winds: prosperity, decline, disgrace, honor, praise, censure, suffering, or pleasure.

But in this incident, she didn't allow Doug to influence her. Instead, she remained based on the point of strength she had developed from her practice. She had clearly made up her mind about what would be right for her and her child and absolutely refused to allow Doug to turn her aside from that. She maintained a proactive stance towards her life, even though he pleaded with her, used his charm—and ultimately his anger —to change her mind.

When living in the lower worlds, each of us can be buffeted by all kinds of circumstances. But as you continue to chant, you will find that you will be overwhelmed by circumstances in life less and less of the time. Ultimately it will be possible to take on anything, without allowing it to discourage and overwhelm you.

Former leaders are good examples of that kind of strength. When Nichiren Daishonin decided to teach this form of Buddhism, he knew that he would be inviting persecution as he would be challenging the beliefs of his day. That didn't dissuade him. Even faced with execution and exile, he remained strong.

In our generation, President Daisaku Ikeda, head of the lay organization of Buddhists, was told by the high priest that he had to step down from the presidency, due to his challenging the corruption of the teachings by the priesthood. He could have given up. Instead he didn't allow it to stop him. He began traveling around the world, starting Buddhist communities where he went. Today, the practice is established in 192 countries.

Being able to remain strong internally when faced with prosperity, decline, disgrace, honor, praise, censure, suffering, and pleasure is one of the great benefits of the practice. Any of these things has the potential to overwhelm your balance, but that strength that develops within will keep you strong in the face of any or all of them.

◢ 32 ◣

Chant and Never Be Deadlocked

Nancy continued chanting that she'd get the job. She added another goal. She wanted a situation where she could be with the baby for periods during the day even though she was working. *You want everything. I wonder if anything like that is even possible.* Now that the baby was kicking the whole idea of being a mother seemed much more real.

Then it hit her. In the back, around a corner from the other offices, there was an unused empty room.

She reflected on the other women working at the agency and tried to remember who had young children. She was pretty sure there were several. Maybe they could go in together and hire someone to watch the children right at work. Warmth filled her heart. That would be absolutely ideal. They'd have to deal with the administration, probably Sue's supervisor, to see if they'd be willing to let them have the space. But first, she was going to have to admit to her pregnancy.

Sitting quietly, she noticed that those little kicks were strengthening. Those kicks meant that soon everyone would guess she was expecting. She couldn't guess what Sue might say when it became obvious.

The next day, Nancy was working at her desk when once again she felt light contractions. Her heart plummeted. Oh no, not now! She couldn't miscarry at work. She got out of her chair and made her way to the ladies' room. Maybe the contractions would just die down like last time, when she'd reduced stress. She rested on the restroom's couch and put up her feet.

Minutes later, Sue entered the restroom. Nancy felt herself blanch. This was all she needed. Sue gave her an inquiring look. "Are you all right?"

Nancy hesitated. Then seeing the compassion in Sue's face, she made a decision. Sue was going to notice her pregnancy soon anyway. It might as well be today. "I thought I should rest for a while. I've been having contractions. I haven't said anything to anybody, but I'm five months pregnant."

Sue nodded. "I've been waiting for you to tell me when you were ready."

Nancy felt a wave of relief. Had Sue suspected the pregnancy when she interviewed her? Hope expanded in her heart. Maybe she wouldn't lose everything.

"Take the time you need," Sue said. "Maybe you should stay home for a day or so."

"I could take some of my paperwork and do it at home," Nancy said. She had to show her worth as an employee.

Sue paused. "You could. Just make sure that everything stays confidential." Sue returned to her office.

Left alone, Nancy considered her living situation. She'd lock the papers in a metal file box where they'd be safe. She was more concerned about what the family would say about her working at all. She didn't want to hear her mother say, "I told you so." She regained her focus. This was up to her, not her mother.

Nancy rested at home the next day, doing as much paperwork as she could. When Sara questioned the wisdom of bringing home work, Nancy gave her one swift look. After that, her sister left the subject alone.

The most stressful thing was not knowing whether she was still in the running for the job now that Sue knew about the pregnancy. To keep herself calm, she chanted a little extra that day.

After returning to work the next morning, Nancy headed in to talk to Sue. She knew she should appear less concerned and more relaxed, but the question was too important. As soon as Sue recognized her and invited her in, Nancy jumped right to the point. "Now that you know about my pregnancy, will it make any difference to my job application?" She waited, every muscle tensed.

Sue shook her head. "Not at all. I was going to contact you today. You've got the job."

A wave of delight followed by a feeling of pride flashed through Nancy. "I couldn't be more pleased," she said, relaxing all over.

Sue smiled warmly. "I feel the same way. I'll be your direct supervisor now. Of course, we will have to work out how to handle the time off you'll need," she said. "You're going to want at least a month with the baby."

"I will," Nancy said. She still didn't know how much money she'd have to work with. "Could you tell me what the salary will be?"

"We're going to start you at $41,500. That's the lower end for that position due to your relative inexperience, but you'll be able to go up from there."

A warm glow settled around Nancy's heart, coupled with a sigh of relief. She was going to be able to support the baby by herself.

Nancy said, "I've been trying to figure out what to do after the month with the baby at home. I've had an idea I wanted to run past you." *Was it too soon to bring this up?* Sue looked inquiring.

Nancy decided to go ahead. *The sooner the better to figure out these arrangements.* "Of the people who work here, how many people have very young children?"

Sue thought for a moment. "Four I think. Sherri, Danielle, Beth and now you."

"If I got the others to agree, could we hire a nanny and use that empty back room around the corner from Human Resources?"

Sue considered the idea. "We don't have any plans for that space right now, but the needs of the agency would have to come first."

Nancy nodded. "Of course. When do you think I could talk to the others about it, to see if it's really feasible?"

"Give me another couple of days. I'll run it by administration." Sue's phone rang and she picked it up. Nancy left quietly.

As she left Sue's office, Nancy walked on air. *I got it! I got the job! Yes!*

She had a feeling deep inside that using the back room for the children would work out, but she couldn't tell what administration would decide. For now, she'd focus her chanting on it and work toward it any way she could. At least Sue hadn't turned her down.

As she neatened her desk in preparation for the new job, Lisa came over. "Are you okay?"

Better than okay. Until Sue announced it, Nancy couldn't tell Lisa about the job. "I've had a couple of scares but the doctor says that as long as things don't get too stressful, everything will be all right."

"And Doug? How are things going with him?"

"I haven't told you, have I?" Nancy said. "His drinking went out of control. I just can't live with it." She sighed. "I had to make a hard decision. I moved out last week and have been living at my sister's."

Lisa gave her a hug. "You're better off without that relationship."

"I've learned a lot about sansho shima," Nancy said ruefully. Lisa raised her eyebrows. Nancy began to explain to Lisa, as Hanako had to her, what sansho shima was and what had happened in her life.

She could hear the district leader say, "Teach to the best of your ability, whether it be just a word or a phrase." One thing she knew now. She could not have taught Lisa anything without having experienced it herself.

The next day, Sue called the team together. Looking around the room she said, "We've closed Annette's position and yesterday we filled it." Everyone looked expectant. Nancy's breathing speeded up.

Sue indicated Nancy. "Nancy will be assuming the position and will begin on Monday." There were murmurs around the room. Nancy noticed that Lisa seemed very pleased. She also saw a frown cross another coworker's face. Not everyone would be delighted. Briefly, she wondered if the coworker had applied for the job. She hoped not. She'd be supervising her.

After the meeting, the members of the team congratulated her. As she accepted their well wishes, she noticed that the same coworker hung back. Nancy could see that there were going to be further challenges to chant about. The difference now was that she knew without doubt that it was possible to overcome them with the practice.

To the Reader

Faith Equals Daily Life

Many people think of religion as something separate from daily life, unrelated from their everyday mundane affairs. You go somewhere, to a retreat or to a place to pray for example, and then return to the world of everyday affairs. Religion is religion; while daily life is daily life.

In Nichiren Buddhism, practitioners view faith and daily life as inseparable. In daily life, we carry out our human revolution and discover and manifest the benefits of the practice.

Does it mean we don't have faith if we have problems? Nichiren Daishonin says that not even saints and sages can avoid problems, so having strong faith doesn't necessarily mean the absence of problems.

"Faith equals daily life" refers to the condition of our interior lives, whether we are strong or weak and whether we can overcome the inevitable problems of life.

This is subtle. For example, if you doubt you have a Buddha nature and don't believe you can solve a problem, then your outer life reflects this belief, and the problem continues to persist. When a shift occurs and you understand you have a Buddha nature and pray accordingly, then your outer life reflects this and the problem resolves.

It doesn't matter what roles we play in life. Our daily lives are the playing field, where we can work through our human revolution and show the benefits of faith.

"Regard your service to your lord as the practice of the Lotus Sutra."

Writings of Nichiren Daishonin , p. 905

In contemporary society, "service to your lord" represents our work as well as all the activities of everyday living. This is where our human revolution takes place .

Nancy is doing this very thing at work. She has worked to transform her inner life, from a person with little drive and lacking in confidence, to someone who is on the way toward making herself a success. To do this, she's had to overcome old habits and fears. For Nancy, who had never spoken up, to go in and present Sue with a proposal was a big step. Other steps included telling Doug how she felt about his drinking and their lives together.

You can see that as Nancy shifted her interior life from passive to proactive, her outer environment reflected these changes by improving as well. She now has a good position where she can truly support herself and the baby. She no longer lives with the stress of sharing her home with an alcoholic. Doug could still start his own ninety-day experiment and, if he stuck with it, change his own karma and attune himself to his Buddha nature as Nancy has done.

When you chant, you also attune your life to your Buddha nature. This allows you to display your potential in the other nine worlds of daily life. Whatever difficulties you're facing you can learn, as Nancy has, to approach each challenge with the confident, determined spirit of a Buddha.

Let's compare your Buddhist practice to the roots of a tree and your daily life as the branches and leaves. If your daily practice becomes inconsistent or weak then your life will reflect this. You can be buffeted by external circumstances, tossed to and fro by the eight winds of life.

But when your daily practice is consistent and strong you come to maintain that inner stability, no matter what happens in your external circumstances.

Some people find they only practice properly when their backs are up against a wall or when they are in crisis. Some examples of crises might be filing for bankruptcy, the sickness of a child, or a partner announcing they want a divorce. Inconsistent practice will deprive a person of the full benefit they can have with daily practice.

If your daily life shows areas of weakness, then ask yourself if you are being consistent and strong in your practice. Remember that faith equals daily life.

⚞33⚟

Who Would Have Believed It!

Over the next couple of months, Nancy settled into her new position and made it her own. She felt much more satisfied in her work.

During October, Nancy visited her obstetrician on a beautiful fall day. She soaked up the sun's warmth, enjoying the Indian summer before the grey of winter arrived. The doctor was having her come more frequently now, as Nancy's due date was only about eight weeks away.

To her great surprise she recognized Annette in the waiting room. *Oh oh, what's she doing here?* Nancy hesitated. How would Annette react to seeing her? She didn't know whether Annette was aware she was the supervisor now, or if Annette would be embarrassed by seeing her.

Nancy reined in her negative thoughts. She had nothing to be ashamed of. She walked over and tentatively smiled.

Annette looked surprised to see her but smiled back. "When are you due?" she asked.

Now, Nancy felt surprised. She had expected Annette to snub her, not ask a friendly question. Annette was nicely dressed and didn't look like a wounded shark anymore. Her former supervisor looked much more relaxed. In fact, Annette looked happy. Nancy found her voice. "I'm due in December. It's a boy."

Annette's eyes sparkled. "That's wonderful," she exclaimed. "When Sue let me go, I was very upset for a couple of weeks. Then, I realized that not having to worry about the job allowed me to do what I had really wanted all along. I just found out I'm pregnant. I'm so happy about it."

Nancy was dumbfounded. She had been chanting for Annette's happiness. Now it had happened.

"When are you due?" she managed to ask.

"In about seven-and-a-half months," Annette actually colored.

"I've got about eight weeks," said Nancy

"Have you gone to birthing classes?" asked Annette. "I'm thinking about it."

Nancy nodded, still incredulous. This was an Annette she had never seen before. She had been unhappy when she was at the agency. Hanako was right. People aren't nasty when they are happy. She couldn't believe the difference.

The receptionist called Annette's name and she picked up her cane and rose to go. She held out her hand. Nancy took it.

Annette was cordial. "Good luck to you. I hope everything goes well with the baby."

"Thanks," Nancy responded. "I hope everything goes well for you, too." To her surprise, Nancy really hoped for Annette's continued happiness.

A few minutes later, Nancy saw her doctor. She was relieved and excited when the doctor said that everything looked normal and right on schedule.

When she got home, she settled herself carefully on the chaise lounge. Who would have ever thought that Annette losing her job would result in her becoming happy? You never knew, when you were chanting about something, how your goal might come about. She marveled at the twists and turns of life. She'd have to tell Sue for sure tomorrow. She'd feel relieved hearing Annette was happy.

Hearing about Annette closed an unfinished chapter in her life. Now she could move on. What were going to be her next steps?

She had the money to find a place of her own now. It was time to move out of her sister's house, so she'd have time to get settled before the baby came.

The chant had strengthened her so that she could protect herself and the baby. She was a practitioner now. She'd proved to her own satisfaction that the practice actually worked and that she wanted it to be her chosen path.

She remembered how, at the newcomer's meeting they'd called it a "prove-it-to-yourself" practice. When she'd first heard that, she hadn't known what it meant. She smiled to herself. She did now.

It seemed fitting to talk with Hanako about getting her own Gohonzon.

Now that she wasn't living with Doug anymore, and she had made it clear she wasn't going back, her new place would be her own environment. It would reflect the person she really was, not who Doug thought she should be. She'd wait to get the Gohonzon until she actually moved into her place. Having it enshrined there would represent the beginning of her new life. Satisfied, she allowed herself to fall asleep.

To the Reader

Receiving the Gohonzon

In the first meeting Nancy attended, she learned that when a person is satisfied with the practice and has decided that they want to commit themselves to this spiritual path, then it would be time to get their own personal Gohonzon for their home.

We have watched Nancy incorporate the practice more and more into her life. Now she relies on it to make difficult decisions. She has come to trust that she will be able to deal with any obstacle that comes up.

She's discovered that when she accesses her deeper wisdom she makes better decisions and understands the issues more clearly. She has also strengthened her self-confidence and is able to stand on her own two feet. She is capable of taking steps that would have been inconceivable only a few months earlier.

As we've seen, some of those steps are not comfortable for her family who have always seen her a certain way. This is not unusual when a person is changing. But, if she persists with the changes, her family or friends will become more comfortable after a period of time.

Often a practitioner isn't aware of his or her own growth. The changes develop in a person's life gradually day by day. If you are doing the ninety-day challenge, you might not see the changes in your own life.

By looking back over a period of time, as Nancy is doing, it will be easier to see how far you've come. Your sponsor will probably have a better idea of your changes than you do. He or she has been watching your growth with great interest from the beginning.

When you have decided that you want to commit yourself to this spiritual path, it's time to let your sponsor know you want your own Gohonzon.

You'll want to start thinking about a good place for your altar. An altar can be set up anywhere that the Gohonzon can be kept safe. If everyone in the family is practicing, the butsudan housing the Gohonzon often ends up in the living room. The practice is the center of family life and the family members all chant together.

If you are living with someone who doesn't practice, and it would be more comfortable and private to have it in a bedroom or in an extra room where you can close the door, that's fine too. The important thing is that you are comfortable, wherever you practice.

You'll have your sponsor and a district leader in your home group who have experience with these things and will advise you. They can visit and evaluate a potential spot with you and then help you set up your altar, so it is there waiting for you to receive your Gohonzon. Then, once you have received it, they will come and make sure it is hung properly, and enshrine it for you.

"The Gohonzon is the clearest of all mirrors, which reflects the entire universe exactly as it is. When you chant to the Gohonzon, you can perceive the true entity of your life and can tap the inexhaustible life force of Buddhahood."

Daisaku Ikeda, *Faith Into Action*, p. 113

◢ 34 ◣

An Aftermath and a Beginning

Epilogue
Twenty Years Later

We've followed Nancy's life from before she met Buddhism to the point where she made the decision to receive her Gohonzon. You have seen how she started the practice and what she had to do to integrate it into her life. You have seen her surmount one obstacle after another as she has become stronger and stronger, while proving the practice to herself.

Now let's return to the community center where we began, and let Nancy relate what happened after she received her Gohonzon.

Nancy leaned forward, holding the sides of the podium. She appeared to have gained energy during the time she had been sharing her life of twenty years of practice. Lights highlighted the butsudan behind her. The vases of greens on either side of it glowed. The audience still listened with interest.

She said, "This evening I've told you what's happened to my life as a result of starting the practice. As a footnote, twenty years ago in December, I gave birth to a healthy baby boy. I've had two more children with my husband, both girls.

I hope that my story encourages all of you. If my life could change the way it has, your life can change for the better too."

The new people looked speculative.

One of them raised her hand. "You've never really told us what happened to Doug," she said.

"That's an important part of the story," Nancy said. "But I can't speak for Doug. Do you want to come up Doug?" She beckoned him forward.

He smiled at her, as he took the microphone. "Nancy has told you what life was like with me when we were living together. I guess we've all had periods of our lives we aren't particularly proud of. The time when I was living with Nancy, and for a short time after, was one of those periods in my life." He turned to Nancy and she nodded back.

"When Nancy told me she was leaving for good it was a wake-up call for me. I realized I loved Nancy. But, first I had to take care of myself."

He looked around the room. "I checked into rehab. That was the beginning of my recovery. AA allows you to choose any spiritual path, so after I sobered up, and saw how Nancy had changed as a result of chanting, I decided I'd try it again. Then I had to accept that she was building her own life for our son, and she wasn't coming back to me. We've co-parented our son Josh and today he's a fine young man.

Eighteen years later I'm still chanting. I am married happily to another woman and am raising two other children. My life is satisfying now." He glanced around the room. "It's been a long evening. Another night I'll tell you what my journey has been like."

He handed the microphone back to Nancy. Waving to the audience, he returned to his seat.

Nancy returned to the podium. With a radiant smile she said, "Each one of you is a Buddha and with the practice you will live a life you can't even imagine now. If someone brought you tonight, he or she will be happy to answer any questions and show you how to get started." She paused briefly and looked around the room. "Thank you so much for coming and taking the time to listen to my story." Glowing, Nancy sat down, relieved to be finished.

The emcee took the microphone. "Thank you all for coming. If you have any questions, anyone here will be happy to answer them."

Several people approached Nancy. A woman started to explain her circumstances. Tears glistened in her eyes. Nancy listened carefully and then reassured her. "The practice will help. Did someone bring you?"

She shook her head.

"Then come back tomorrow night to a new people's meeting." She put an arm around the woman's shoulder and turned to another practitioner. "Would you make sure she gets a copy of *The Winning Life*?" She turned to the newcomer. "I'll see you at the meeting." The woman nodded, gave Nancy a shy smile and followed the practitioner to the bookstore.

Nancy watched them go. Twenty years ago she'd been that person. And look where she was now. A quiet joy filled her. She looked forward to following the lives of these new people. Watching their lives turn around was very satisfying. Who knows, she thought. In a few years, maybe one of them would be giving this talk.

To the Reader

Summarizing the Main Points

This book was written to show you how to use the practice in your daily life. Anyone who establishes a consistent practice can become happy. Toward that end, let's review the main concepts which are the stepping stones to establishing a solid practice.

You Have a Buddha Nature

All of us have a Buddha nature, although most are unaware of it. Once you bring it out in your life, you can live a life of unshakeable happiness and freedom endowed with great energy and a deep wisdom.

- Your Buddha nature connects you with all of life in the depths of your being.

- You suffer because you are trying to build your happiness on transient things, temporary happiness. It is possible to build unshakeable happiness from the inside out, no matter what happens in your external environment.

- You can tap the wisdom and life force of your Buddha nature by chanting Nam-myoho-renge-kyo, which will allow you to overcome obstacles that have prevented you from being happy.

Prove the practice to Yourself

Remember this is a "prove-it-to-yourself-practice." Nancy was presented with the ninety day-challenge to pick a concrete goal that was a stretch and chant for it for ninety days.

Review of the Guidelines for Goal Setting

- Make sure your goal reflects what you want, not what you don't want.
- Plan to chant twice a day to keep your life in tune with the rhythm of the universe.
- There will be temptations to skip chanting, maybe from family or circumstances. Be true to yourself and chant anyway. Don't take the easy way out.
- Chant with determination (this is what I want and I'm willing to take action and do whatever is necessary to get it), rather than just hoping, but not believing it will really happen. You will have much better results.
- There can be three outcomes to chanting for your goal.
  1. You will get what you are chanting for, a benefit.
  2. The benefit may be obvious, a conspicuous benefit or it may be inconspicuous, such as growth in character. You might not achieve the goal but you will understand why that outcome benefits you more.
  3. Finally, you may get the benefit and it will lead to some awakening in some area of your life.

To Overcome Obstacles and Challenges

Always remember, it is your birthright to be happy. The practice exists to allow you to become enlightened and to overcome the negative circumstances in your life which are making you unhappy. When you are faced with some of those circumstances try the following:

- Remind yourself you can transform any negative circumstance into a positive outcome through the practice. This is "turning poison into medicine."

- When you chant for your goal, pay particular attention to ideas which come to you concerning the goal. Also pay attention to "coincidences" which are moving you toward your goal.
- Take action on the ideas you receive.
- When you chant, you can raise your internal state of life and overcome fears and anxieties so you can move forward with your goals.
- When you face a big obstacle don't be discouraged. Remember that overcoming obstacles is the path to enlightenment and unshakeable happiness. You have to go through them as they are blocking your happiness.
- You can never be deadlocked if you continue to chant for your goal.
- Chant until you receive your goal. Sometimes this is rapid, sometimes it takes weeks or months. But it will eventually happen as long as you don't give up.

Stay Close to More Experienced Practitioners

If you have doubts, get discouraged or have experiences you don't understand, go to a meeting or ask the person who introduced you. You will need the support of the more experienced practitioners. You can borrow their certainty until you have the experiences which will build your own faith. They can also make sure you're focusing your chanting for the best results.

Practice to Achieve Your Human Revolution

- Always practice the strategy of the Lotus Sutra and chant about something before strategizing. After doing so, you will have greater wisdom when you think about your circumstances.

- If you face a crucial moment, chant with focus and intensity for what you want until you feel relaxed about the outcome.

- Always remember that to change our circumstances, we must change ourselves. The circumstances of our lives, our unique environment, reflect the state of our inner lives.

- You are changing past karma. Congratulations!

- As you overcome your weaknesses and accomplish your human revolution your whole life will change for the better. It's not easy, but it's worth it.

- As you become unshakeably happy from the inside out, you will become immune to the ups and downs of life, —the eight winds.

- This is a practice for self and others so teach others to the best of your ability and help others to become happy.

"Now that you have finished my book, won't you please consider writing a short review? Reviews help readers discover great new books. I would truly appreciate it. Just go to www.amazon.com/books. Then put Margaret Blaine in Search."

Bibliography

References for books quoted, below.

Daishonin, Nichiren, *The Writings of Nichiren Daishonin, vols 1& 2.* **Tokoyo 160-8583, Japan. Soka Gakkai, 2006.**

Hochswender, Woody, Martin, Greg, Marino, Ted, *The Buddha in Your Mirror, Practical Buddhism and the Search for Self.* **Santa Monica, California: Middleway Press, 2001.**

Ikeda, Daisaku, *Faith into Action.* **Santa Monica, California; World Tribune Press, 1999.**

Ikeda, Daisaku, *Buddhism Day by Day, Wisdom for Modern Life.* **Santa Monica , California: Middleway Press, 2006.**

Soka Gakkai, *The Soka Gakkai Dictionary of Buddhism,* **Soka Gakkai 32 Shinanomachi, Shinjuku-ku, Tokyo, Japan, 2002.**

How to Find Us

On the website www.sgi-usa.org, there is a list of the major centers in the United States. Put in your zip code to find a group in your area.

The sole purpose of the *Soka Gakkai* is the happiness of the members, so don't be shy about calling. People in the group will welcome you.

Volunteers in any of those centers will be able to direct you to the center closest to you. The national centers will probably be open during the day. Local centers are run by volunteers who usually are available in the evenings. Sometimes the closest group to you is a district and the district leader will be the person contacting you.

On this website there is an online store where you can find reading material and audio tapes on Nichiren Buddhism.

Other Resources

www.margaretblaine.com

About Margaret Blaine

Margaret Blaine practiced as a licensed clinical social worker for 25 years, working with people from all walks of life, with a wide variety of problems. She saw all kinds of human suffering, mental health issues, battered women, child and family problems, and many types of relationship problems. She often wondered if there was anything which could help people to become happy.

In 1994 she was introduced to Nichiren Buddhism and went to meetings to learn about the philosophy and daily chanting practice. There she heard the experiences of hundreds of people, who were experienced practitioners. Some had been stuck in their lives and had broken through the blockage and moved forward. Others had overcome obstacles and problems in all areas of life. They had surmounted major transitions in their lives, achieved impossible goals, found perfect places for themselves in work and life, and become happy.

Seeing and hearing experiences like this, she was galvanized and wanted to know more. Margaret started the daily chanting practice herself, and found that her own life shifted into work uniquely suited to her and became richly satisfying.

Since then, she has worked in an Oregon Prison, taught prisoners how to chant, and has focused on making Buddhism accessible to newcomers through writing the book, setting up a website, and guiding newcomers into the chanting practice.

Margaret lives in Eugene Oregon with her husband. She has three children and grandchildren. Retired from counseling she enjoys writing, physical fitness, gardening, playing the piano, and working in her local Buddhist group.

BONUS DOWNLOAD
For readers of this book

The Key Steps to Chanting

Get your copy here:

www.margaretblaine.com/keysteps